THE QUEST

THE QUEST

Helping Our Children Find Meaning and Purpose

Harlan Carl Scheffler

GR

GEORGE RONALD PUBLISHER
OXFORD

George Ronald, *Publisher*
Oxford
www.grbooks.com

ISBN: 978-0-85398-503-7
0-85398-503-0

Illustrations by the author

Acknowledgement is made to the following for use of copyrighted illustrations:
Sovran Bank, N.A., 186
Kraft Foods, Inc.: page 24
Dynamic Graphics, Inc.: pages 13, 16, 19, 25, 29, 31, 34, 43, 45

Part 1 of this book is also published separately as
Challenge: Helping our Children Find Meaning and Purpose,
ISBN 978-0-85398-506-8
0-85398-506-5

A catalogue record for this book is available from the British Library

Printed and bound by Biddles Ltd, King' s Lynn, Norfolk

CONTENTS

In remembrance of ‘Abdu’l-Bahá

****

For my parents, May and Carl Scheffler

****

I wish to thank
Helen Sousa, Dr. Victor deAraujo, Betty deAraujo,
Hank Swain, Tab Low, Vic Bachman, and Marva Snyder
Their assistance with the words and the meanings
is deeply appreciated.

And to my wife, Barbara:
I thank you for your love,
your abiding patience,
and your pure heart.

The Search for Truth

One of the essays from the old file

In the endeavor to become re-oriented toward the realities that constitute true civilization, we must have courage to face facts in all areas of life and thought. To hold reservations in any instance would inevitably defeat us. This is a challenge that not many may be really prepared to make.

Since every person takes part in the social life of his environs, he also bears direct responsibility for whatever may be developed. Its successes are to a degree his, but so are its failures. Every facet of human activity inevitably interlocks all human thought and action. For this reason it is not possible to disregard any activity or interest that plays a role in the social order.

Civilization inevitably rests upon the individuals who constitute the masses in any time or place. Each person through his personal reaction contributes toward the mores that constitute the physical, intellectual, and spiritual or moral climate of society. And since all contribute, it is logical that they are responsible, and it also gives each the right to determine what that relation should be. Thus he is placed in the position of responsibility, as well as independence, and for this reason he must not blindly accept the effects of religious, educational, or other conclusions, without weighing them carefully and objectively. Blind acceptance of the word of any other man, be he learned or ignorant, automatically deprives a person of truth. Simply because he accepts it blindly.

We must also recognize that ultimately Truth must be one thing. It is not something that is divided. In science we have learned that we must have a flexible attitude toward what comprises scientific knowledge, because as scientists we are always opening new doors to new and wider understanding, but we haven't obtained absolute truth.

A similar attitude toward every other facet of human life would undoubtedly open the door to wider horizons in every other area. This is important in education, and it must apply to religion as well.

Excerpt from *Purpose* by Carl Scheffler (1935)

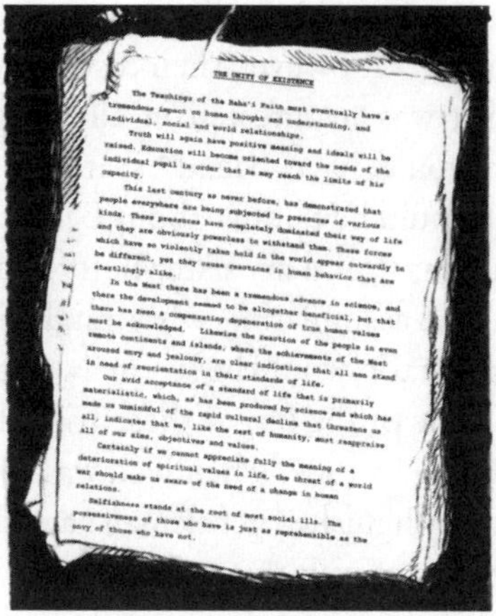

THE UNITY OF EXISTENCE

The Teachings of the Baha'i Faith must eventually have a tremendous impact on human thought and understanding, and individual, social and world relationships.

Truth will again have positive meaning and ideals will be raised. Education will become oriented toward the needs of the individual pupil in order that he may reach the limits of his capacity.

This last century as never before, has demonstrated that people everywhere are being subjected to pressures of various kinds. These pressures have completely dominated their way of life and they are obviously powerless to withstand them. These forces which have so violently taken hold in the world appear outwardly to be different, yet they cause reactions in human behavior that are startlingly alike.

In the West there has been a tremendous advance in science, and there the development seemed to be altogether beneficial, but that there has been a compensating degeneration of true human values must be acknowledged. Likewise the reaction of the people in even remote continents and islands, where the achievements of the West aroused envy and jealousy, are clear indications that all men stand in need of reorientation in their standards of life.

Our avid acceptance of a standard of life that is primarily materialistic, which, as has been produced by science and which has made us unmindful of the rapid cultural decline that threatens us all, indicates that we, like the rest of humanity, must reappraise all of our aims, objectives and values.

Certainly if we cannot appreciate fully the meaning of a deterioration of spiritual values in life, the threat of a world war should make us aware of the need of a change in human relations.

Selfishness stands at the root of most social ills. The possessiveness of those who have is just as reprehensible as the envy of those who have not.

Prologue

While sorting through my parent's papers and personal records some years ago, I came across an old metal-clasped paperboard file. The contents, innumerable pages, many handwritten, others painstakingly typed on fragile onionskin by my mother, were manuscripts composed by my father. Most were numbered and held fast with rusty paper clips, and a few were orphans detached from their sequence. These essays, never published, treated the most unusual of subjects: 'The Relationship of Truth to Human Life', 'Being Purposeful', 'The Unity of Existence', 'Human Values'. Over the years these compositions, tucked away in the ancient file, were apparently locked as well in my slumbering consciousness. Every so often I would open the metal fastening and leaf through the sheaves, musing about those earlier and unpretentious times when people were disposed to concern themselves with such thoughts. And for me to find these papers, and then find them again, bothering me to see and to touch, has developed into a kind of intriguing search.

During the passage of my formative years, it gradually dawned on me that I had been assigned to an unusual family. My parents, born and raised in midwest America, grew up with early nineteenth-century values. My father was a teacher and artist; my mother, a homemaker.* However, their discovery of the principles of the Bahá'í Faith was manifested in all aspects of their lives. Oftentimes they would have friends seated around the supper table, and they all would be talking about Bahá'u'lláh and 'Abdu'l-Bahá and the 'Teachings', and my sister Betty and I would sit there quietly, listening and assimilating what might be assimilated. It would be later that we too would be swept away by these concepts.

Our father was one of the few at these friendly gatherings who had met 'Abdu'l-Bahá. In 1907, when Dad was 24 years old, he and an older and most distinguished gentleman named Thornton Chase travelled across the sea to visit this turbaned man from the East. At that time, 'Abdu'l-Bahá was incarcerated in the prison-city of 'Akká, Palestine. The chronicle of His and His father's lives is a record of persecution and exile and imprisonment lasting over fifty years. The history of these two remarkable personages, and the impact of their lives, comprise a moving and fascinating account of the dramatic beginnings of what is evolving to be the resurgence of the renewal of faith. It is now obvious to me that the gatherings at our table and the joyous conversations were in response to this impact. Undoubtedly the writings of 'Abdu'l-Bahá and the documentation of His talks – talks delivered to small groups and large assemblies in America and Europe after He was freed from incarceration – were designed for everyone, but certainly they were to appeal to people like me – or we were destined for them.

From early on, I was a youngster obsessed with the nature of things, why things work as they do. How can the caterpillar turn into a butterfly – what miracle is taking place as I watch the time-lapse photography reveal this puzzling phenomenon? What transcendental transformation is happening to the lowly caterpillar as its chrysalistic protoplasmic mush begins to manufacture legs, wings, and antennae? It wasn't enough to be told, 'Well, that's just the way it works.' I had to know more. 'Abdu'l-Bahá's writings, treating the

* See page 194.

complexities of existence with profound but uncomplicated insight, aligning the structures of the 'material' to a partnership with the 'spiritual', present a rare insight into the mysteries of life. Both those who place trust in omniscience and belief, and those who give authority to science and reason, will find His dissertations relevant.

Perhaps biology would have been a better field for me, but I became an artist. This engraving was made when I was working at a studio in Chicago. In between drawings of hamburgers and ladies' cosmetics, I found time to render this portrait of 'Abdu'l-Bahá.

My reference was an early photograph taken in Dublin, New Hampshire, when 'Abdu'l-Bahá was visiting America in 1912. The engraving took quite a while, as it was put aside when job assignments came my way. A friend and co-worker, Fernando Da Silva (Fred), had casually watched my progress as the drawing developed. He was a fine illustrator; his knowledge of the natural harmony and conformity of the human figure was held in high regard, so, when this work was nearing completion, I brought it to Fred for his comment. He looked and studied as I waited anxiously for some advice, and then he backed away and said quietly, almost whispering to himself, 'How kind, so kind . . .'

And Fred was right. 'Abdu'l-Bahá was a man who had compassion for the forgotten and the deprived. Children somehow found happiness when near Him.

Although kind and giving, 'Abdu'l-Bahá was firm in the proclamation of the principles He espoused. And He was vigilant in defining His own capacity with regard to these teachings. His insights are the exemplification of His Father Bahá'u'lláh's teachings. As exalted and soul-stirring as these explanations might be, and as forthright as was His bearing, it was 'Abdu'l-Bahá, Himself, who touched the heart of the common person. During the latter years of His imprisonment, those who were in charge of His confinement found it impossible not to accord Him extraordinary courtesy and even reverential esteem. My father would recall the contradictory behaviour of the jailers, who, when leaving 'Abdu'l-Bahá's presence, would lower their heads and bow as they backed away. Strange as it might seem to us today, this remarkable man from Persia was addressed as 'Master'.

The observations outlined in this book are my understanding of these writings and explanations, and nothing more. In one of His discourses, 'Abdu'l-Bahá invites us all to think about these concepts and discover our own perspective. It is implied that once the key to understanding is discovered, there are many meanings waiting to be disclosed. What fun! Then I'll read your book! In the meantime, I hope that you enjoy mine.

PART ONE

CHALLENGE

Introduction

We all are talking about how the world is changing and how it used to be. Our parents and grandparents tell us stories about their childhood and how family was the focus of their lives, and community was the centre. Home, church, and school were their fortress. Today we fear we have lost the connections, and sense that this is reflected in our, and our children's, lives. We hardly ever sit together around the table and share and laugh. Probably much of this disassociation started when we left the farm and headed for the city – for those bright new horizons. We quickly became less connected to the family and the community, and certainly to the land itself. We thought we were designed to be self-sufficient creatures, that independence was a show of strength. Now, however, we find we are transients, just passing through, touching down here and there with our connections. Friendships and commitments are oftentimes tenuous, and there is little that connects us with fundamentals.

Though, regrettably, we may have distanced ourselves from those simpler times, technology connects us to the far corners of the world, and we instantly have a relationship to every other person and every other event, as though distance were not a factor at all. Today, we are so closely linked that we cannot escape our interdependence and, for that matter, our accountability. There can be no doubt that the consequences of our actions, perhaps even our thoughts, mysteriously impact on others with whom we have no direct association. The chain and networking of causes and effects extends in all directions and consequently we are, as well, the recipients of countless nearby and far-off initiatives. Comfortably seated at a computer viewing the screen and pushing a button, with our cup of coffee or Pepsi-Cola a like movement-of-the-hand away, no doubt we are connected, in the technological sense, but, tragically, we are often not involved with others – not truly connected. Things have changed.

My wife, Barbara, tells of the time when she was invited to a 'newcomers' gathering in our suburban neighborhood. She was warmly greeted by the hostess with the question, 'How long are you going to be here?' 'Just long enough for tea and cookies' was not the right answer. Most of the women knew their husbands would be moved on by their corporate jobs in a few months or years.

This small book attempts to bring into focus the inherent *oneness of things*; how we, as parts of the whole, naturally intertwine with each other and with all the environments that embrace us. Our isolation, whether racial, religious, societal, or ecological, is a very real obstacle that continues to block the way to our achieving this unifying and all-encompassing goal. Most disturbing is the impression of normality we are giving our young people, implying with our resignation and, unfortunately, our complacency, that things are the way they are, and there is nothing we can do about it. Our fragile connection with the surrounding systems, coupled with our worldwide and unrelenting distrust of each other, present problems that appear to be beyond our resources to resolve. As individuals, tied down as we are by obligations and responsibilities at home and at work, we wonder what we can do to effect change and create a better world for our children. We wait for our leaders to lead the way, but they are too busy reacting to a course of events that has its own agenda. Caught up in the torrent of an evolutionary process beyond our control, we appear powerless to direct our own destiny, able only to organize our comparatively mundane affairs as the mainstream surges forward. Our free will is a petty power when measured against the unfolding of some predestined plan.

It is true that we are the ones who can critically analyse our own state of affairs, come to conclusions, and change our ways. We can vow this and resolve to do that, but if the developing circumstances call for a different resolution from the one we have chosen, our progress is interrupted, perhaps aborted, and we become frustrated and disheartened. If, for example, we legislate and work to accommodate the requirements of a tribal or national goal, when all along the demands for our survival are attuned to the needs of a more encompassing social and mental/spiritual environment, our efforts will be without fruition. If we refuse to acknowledge the inviolability of a preordained course that disciplines our advancement, our shortsighted perception will fail to align our energies with the imperatives of larger, more expansive objectives, and we will find we are constantly fighting the natural flow. The cave dweller could not foresee the tribe, although the fortunes and vicissitudes of his daily life directed him, without his awareness, toward this greater security. Even though the recorded chapters of our history detail the wars and revolutions that have accompanied our progress, proof enough that we resisted what could have been the natural, gradual, and peaceful evolution of society, the chronicle itself is the epic story of our development toward more universal goals. From nomad and even earlier, to now, the irreversible

direction and incontrovertible nature of our progress brings an awareness that we are caught up in the evolution of a great movement, and heading toward the fulfilment of its purpose.

How our children fit into this unfolding is outlined in this small book. Part 1 outlines the challenges and proposes broad solutions, while Parts 2 to 5 examine these more closely. How the children, as distinct and particular parts of the present evolution, contribute to the functioning and fruition of the whole is a vital consideration if they are to understand the significance of their lives. The disciplines that define the relationship and responsibility of the individual to the entirety are, it will be explained, relative not only to the organization of the components of the physical world, but to the regulatory laws of the non-physical, spiritual, world as well. An inquiry into the nature of existence and the role people play as participants, contributing to the oneness, is the commission evolution is assigning to our children.

As caring parents and teachers, ourselves children of the half-light, faintly perceiving the dawning and radiance of the era that lies ahead, we have our own tasks to perform. These entail responsibilities to our children that are essential and weighty, and require a great amount of sacrifice. It is clear that we must not only devote time and attention to this commitment, but we must take care that our own attitudes do not impair their freedom to participate in this wonderful new day. An unrelenting tenacity that bonds us to outdated systems is inappropriate at any stage of society's development, but especially today when all of mankind is struggling with the same transformation. As our hopes and dreams are embodied in the children's future, our greatest fear is that our well-intentioned guidance may fail to equip them to function with relevance in their evolving world. Our fascination with the superficial, the mean and trivial; our inflexible social, racial, and religious prejudicial inclinations, and our relegation of spirituality to a separate facet of life will, in all likelihood, not facilitate their journey.

The precious gift we are free to give is the opportunity for our children to participate in their own world – a world we older folks did not and could not know. Tying them to our perceptions, perhaps using them to relive our own lives, is not fair. If we find this assignment just too difficult, *let us look carefully at the faces and into the eyes of our children – the world's children*. Here clearly and truly we can see the wondrous homogeneity that is inherently shared by all. These beautiful young people, mirroring the oneness of humanity, innocent, uncommitted, and gifted with unknowable promise, are waiting for enlightenment. They are also vulnerable, available to any influence. Committed to be worthy of their trust, we had best be attentive and alert to the responsibility we have assumed. The consequences of our choices in nurturing and guiding these untouched and receptive minds are momentous. Whether in the home or the classroom, the workplace or the community, it is obvious that accountability for their security falls upon us. It is for this reason that the principles we teach must be fundamental and true, so that our children can have one criterion with which to measure all things. The evolution of the human race moves forward with the enhancement of each new generation, and the sacrifice of the parents is imperative, in seeing that the capacities of the children are free to reflect the influence of the new era as it unfolds. Today, the special and underlying principle that will enable the children to find their way is the disclosure that existence, including, of course, each precious child, is essentially a non-physical reality. This reappraisal and reassignment will ultimately reveal a new creation and a new world. Beauty and majesty will adorn all forms and will grace the lives of each and every child.

There is a warning implied. If the concerns of mankind are not protected and monitored by the same postulate that directs the established ordering of life, the natural energy flowing through us will be arbitrary, and society will reflect the blatant and unbounded evidences of dysfunctionality and negativity that we witness today.

****

After all these years, Barbara and I still have our Friday night date. One evening, not so long ago, we were looking forward to supper at 'Europa', a quaint old-world German restaurant known for its spaetzle and sauerbraten. By chance, this particular occasion was to be favoured with the performance of a costumed alpine yodeller with his accordion. While we were enjoying our meal, another couple entered the room with their small child and were seated at the table next to us. It didn't take long for this cute 2-year-old tot to catch the spirit. Sitting in his booster chair, listening to the music, he waved his arms and swayed his little body, laughing with delight. German fried potatoes were furthest from *his* mind. He just couldn't sit still and couldn't hear and feel enough. Right there, before our eyes, Barbara and I saw the miracle happen! He and the music became one.

That happy youngster could not have realized the importance of that encounter – how that musical interlude would mark his life (perhaps) *forever*. Particularly when we are little, we are like sponges, soaking up every increment that will define our being. And then when we are old, we will have a story to tell. This is especially true for those of us who are to witness this remarkable accelerating period of our history. We cannot know how *this* little fellow found his way, whether or not he is playing his accordion and yodelling his heart out in some alpine Swiss chalet, but just for fun let me tell you what happened to me.

Connections

In 1922, when I took my place in the course of human affairs, the world was very different. The span of a lifetime such as mine was to witness unprecedented milestones. The beginnings of technology and the downfall of isolationism apparently were destined to take place in this microsecond of our history – can you imagine! I was the child who toyed with the crystal set, touching the needle to connect with the hidden sounds, and I was the youngster turning the pages of the *National Geographic*, wondering about the remote lands and peoples, pondering the strange countenances caught in a moment of time.

I can hardly believe I survived the perils of those days. Collecting mercury from broken thermometers and rolling the lethal ball in the palm of my hand was an adventure, but watching its offspring come into existence with a tap of my finger was, I thought, a miracle. Melting cubes of lead over the gas flame on my mother's stove and molding the heavy liquid to create cowboys and Indians, carving smooth the seams with silvery-gray fingers, was fun. And I'm still here to tell how my dad and I would go to Hendrick's Drug Store and buy chunks of potassium cyanide to dispatch beetles and butterflies for my collection (hopefully painlessly). Gracious!

And now I am seated at my computer, connected intimately with the world. I know now, but I didn't know then: listening and touching and looking was my introduction to the mystical world of insight.

Learning about the two worlds – the material one and the more-than-material one – started when I was very young. Nature always interested me. How can the caterpillar turn into a butterfly? What makes things work? Vacations in the North Woods, trips to the Natural History Museum and Aquarium and Planetarium were part of the undisclosed agenda my parents had planned for my sister Betty and me. How life, in all of its aspects, presents itself, was the exciting fundamental of my parents' teaching. Had they not shared this secret, my sister and I would have most likely travelled our paths unmindful and unaware. As a family, we went about our business of work and play, but inwardly our lives were directed by the oneness of this wondrous material/non-material partnership. It was the central *theme* that paved our way. Hence, when as a youngster I was on my bicycle heading for the forest preserve to poke around in the ponds and streams, or, much later, caring for the wounded on a hospital ship in the South Pacific, my true home was in the non-physical world.

How my bicycle and the forest pond and the countless other happenstances of my life served to connect me with the non-physical side of things is a mystery, but certainly not just my mystery. We all **physically** connect with the so-called *immaterial* world:

- The **eye** looks, enabling *sight*, and sight welcomes ***perception***.
- The **ear** hears, but *listening* is more, and ***meaning*** is even more.
- The **finger** touches, but *feeling* is revealed, and then ***distinction***.
- The **tongue** tastes, taste summons *flavour*, and ***discernment*** is born.
- The **nose** smells, but *scent* is invited to reveal ***sensitivity***.

Our physical tools allow the non-physical realities to become known, and with our ability to attribute significance to the signs displayed, our own true identity comes forward.

My teachers at Haven School were well prepared to teach the magic of numbers and letters, but the deeper meanings, toward which these lessons could have led, were not addressed. And Haven School was not alone.

From the outset, our children are introduced to a divided world, a world where material things are true, and intangible, non-material considerations are also true. The problem for our youngsters is to figure out how, in the classroom, two truths can be in contention with each other (or apparently so, for one can be taught, and the other cannot). There must be some flaw in our thinking, and how and what we are teaching, for reason tells us that there can be only one truth; truth isn't one thing – which can also be two. Where are the experts who might help the children with this conundrum?

As parents and guardians (teachers), let us not underestimate our own competence. If truth is one, then we must look again at what *we* have been taught and told, and find the flaw ourselves.

Affinity Abounds

Since the dawning of intellect, the quest to uncover the fundamentals of life has been the mission of the inquiring mind. Long before technology was to make its appearance, thoughtful thinkers were thinking thoughtful thoughts. After our species had fulfilled the requisites of our physical, intellectual, and societal evolution – a germination spread over countless epochs and eras – a Greek philosopher named Democritus came on the scene. He theorized that if matter were divided into smaller and smaller pieces, it would eventually reach a point where it could no longer be divided. This smallest bit of matter was called *átoms*, a Greek word meaning 'not cuttable'. This Greek idea about the nature of matter was then largely forgotten for more than 2,000 years. Then in 1803 John Dalton, an English scientist, proposed a theory about atoms. He believed that all elements are made up of these minuscule particles, which *cannot be created* or *destroyed* or even split. He thought that atoms of the same element are alike, and differ from atoms of any other element. Dalton also believed that different atoms combine in definite ratios to form molecules.

Two hundred years have passed since John Dalton shared his thoughts. Along the way, other scientists have submitted their theories, some, even, have split the atom, but still we are not privileged to understand the true essence – the inner workings – of this mysterious atomic entity. But there are clues. Life hints at its secrets.

Science has determined that the atom is the key factor enabling existence to become known. It is the basic component of every physical form, past, present and future; known and unknown. All the categories of life, herein named mineral, vegetable, animal and human 'kingdoms', employ these complex particles to present their substances and identities to the world of being. And to make things even more confusing, we are told that the atom's composition is less (or more, if you like) than 'material'. If we were to examine the integral parts of every definable form – elephant tooth, cup of coffee, or whatever – we would find (up to the time of this writing) no more than 110 elements – in total, the basic substance of life. All of existence is made up of these essential fundamental ingredients. And each element takes its place in this miraculous display through the participation of its smallest particles – its atoms. A mere few, particularized and gathered together in the structure of our DNA, enable our genetic heritage. In addition, we are told that the atoms themselves are constructed of electrified sub-particles, some charged positively, some charged negatively, and (of course) some with no electrical charge at all. It is here that our perception of our substantial world and our bodily selves becomes fuzzy, sort of illusionary, because these tiny bits of matter are themselves a bit ambiguous. They assume a disguise, for they do not fit into the physical slot as much as we would like. So, way back in history, when we were beginning to examine our surroundings and wonder about ourselves, our linguistic experts designed a word that helped explain things, and that word is **energy**. Energy defines the atom and is its attribute.

Attribute! Where did we find this one? What a wonderful word! And why so wonderful? Wonderful because it serves to define a non-physical condition and presence. *Non-physical attributes define all physical matter*; can you imagine. In the mineral realm, a rock is a rock because its atoms hold together and form a structure, and we name this holding-together-attribute *cohesion*. It is a *non-physical* quality, and it identifies the essence of the rock. We can pick up a rock, bur we cannot pick up cohesion. We can examine a rock, bur we cannot examine cohesion.

What is the difference between a plastic rose (or a dead one) and a real live rose? Well, one is just an assortment of mineral atoms dressed up in fancy attire busily demonstrating *cohesion*, and the other is an assortment of mineral atoms busily showing off not only cohesion, but *growth* and *metabolism* as well. None of these attributes have substantial presence, but they are essential in identifying the substantial presence of the rose. A rose cannot be known without knowing its non-physical qualities and attributes.

An incomprehensible configuration of specific mineral atoms (*live* mineral atoms!) appropriately assembled in the form of a small house mouse, *evokes* a small house mouse, because the house mouse configuration enables *cohesion*, *growth*, *sense perception* and *instinct* to become manifested – all defining attributes.

And how it could be, and who could imagine, that our own minuscule atoms, packed tight with energy, might work in concert to facilitate a *harmonious thought* or the *freedom to choose*?

The Great Mystery

The greatest mystery of all, of course, is that all the different forms – employing the same atoms and displaying the same energy – behave so differently. It is an unusual consideration, but it is quite obvious that a particular material composition cannot but evoke a predictable non-physical performance. The way things are put together will determine how they will behave.

In theory, if our children in their science class could introduce a few more than 66 billion billion atoms of hydrogen to a smattering of more than 33 billion billion atoms of oxygen, they would bring forth one drop of water. And if the children could combine a determined assortment of these tiny particles, assemble and align them just as they are so perfectly assembled and aligned in the petunia, they would create a petunia. The effect is already in the cause. There is not even a remote chance that a honeybee will write a sonnet – even though its atoms are the same as ours.

So let's give energy a round of applause and honour it with a capital 'E', for it is the answer to our dilemma. Here lies the flaw in our thinking, for we have placed Energy in the wrong slot. Good old-fashioned Energy – it makes the material world, and the more-than-material world, one. Good old non-physical Energy!

We can help our children understand how Energy, fundamental, inexplicable, unknowable, but true, proves its own existence. In the classroom, if our students were given a bundle of atoms to hold in their cupped hands, and it had shape only, they would quickly identify it as a mineral of some kind – a chunk of limestone or granite. If the assembled particles were growing, perhaps photosynthesizing, the children would easily name this assortment an aster or asparagus. If the sample were furry and cute and purred, they would call it a kitten. And, though too large to hold in cupped hands, if the conglomeration was thinking and hopping about and trusting and loving and wondering about things, they would be looking at themselves. In the guise of atoms selected from that warehouse of 110 elements, our faithful friend Energy is doing its job of bringing forth miracles.

And then the questions will start. 'How can the same atoms display so many different attributes?' 'Surely these tiny particles are not able to make choices, decide when to hold on to one another, or grow, or move around or think about things?' David will join in, 'And how do they know when to come on the scene and when to leave?' And Kara will raise her hand and wonder, aloud, 'If Energy appears in all these life forms without their beckoning or approval, who or what is responsible?' Well, Kara, the answer to this question is not to be found in your textbook. It is a very good question, but one that you will be better able to address as you get older and as you mature. Your Maths, Science, Social Studies, Languages, Arts and History lessons are the necessary tools of learning, and, as you acquire knowledge, be assured that insight will follow. However, it will not follow unless you ask lots of questions along the way.

'Questions? Questions about what?' Kara, questions about everything!

Cause and Effect

The physical compositions of all life forms define and determine the degree of Energy that is to be displayed. Non-physical Energy, pure and simple, does not and cannot reveal its full power, for its measure is eclipsed by the capacities that reflect it. The mineral, vegetable, animal and human kingdoms, perfectly formed as they are, impose restrictions. In its secret world, the mineral might wish to fly, but that is a futile wish.

Well, this isn't quite true. What does the teacher answer when Sylvie wonders: 'When the sparrow takes a drink of water, and those atoms of oxygen and hydrogen become sparrow and the sparrow flies away, aren't the minerals flying? And when the cow eats the grass, and the grass turns into cow, can we say that the mineral and vegetable particles can now moo?' And after Sylvie has had time to muse about her musings, she might present her paper with this observation: 'If the same atoms are used over and over again by the different life forms, and these compositions determine the degree of Energy that is to be displayed, then Energy must have a life of its own. If this were not so, we would have to credit the atoms themselves with this initiative – that they are in control of their own destiny and can, if they choose, lift themselves up by their own bootstraps.'

In their discussion class, the children might tackle the relationship between cause and effect. What an interesting topic! Somewhere along the way they might discover that *cause* and *effect* are so closely linked that they change places with each other – the effect becomes the cause of the next effect – immediately, without a perceptible lapse of time. The relationship is so fixed that the children can plan every action with confidence and direct every thought with predictability.

And then there is another consideration. A cause cannot enter or become a part of its effect – it *creates* the effect. Energy, as the cause, does not become a large flower or a small elephant, nor does Energy paint marvellous works of art. Rather, non-physical Energy uses the physical forms (minerals, plants, animals and people) as intermediaries to bring forth its non-physical effects (attributes).

And then another observation might come to mind. Perfection is an attribute of life; all beings, minerals included, reflect the presence of Energy perfectly. (We must stop telling the mineral kingdom it is dead. We search the outer regions of the universe, hoping to find signs of life, forgetting that the atoms in the most distant galaxy are dancing.) However, perfection is relative, not absolute. Thus, the rock holds together perfectly; the flower grows in exemplary fashion; the pollywog's wiggly ways are flawless, and the child is inimitable. Everything manifests Energy perfectly, to the degree allotted to and allowed by its parent kingdom. The premise here outlined suggests that the differences in our children have little to do with their essentiality, their intrinsic nature, for their Energy is essence-mixed with the quintessence (or the word of your choosing) of life. When a child is conceived, the mix of atoms and molecules and genes – the components of egg and sperm – impose restrictions on the degree of Energy that is allowed, and it is in this manner that the child's capacities and aptitudes come into being. Although the propensities for specialization and uniqueness (personality, too) are concealed therein, these attributes will gradually become apparent as the little one sets out on his or her journey. We must remind ourselves: the child is something more than – and something apart from – his or her attributes. Attributes describe the child, bur they are not the child.

Energy has been around forever, but until we came on the scene, pictures and images, descriptions and depictions, were abiding in the secret world waiting to be born. Then, in due course and after the passage of the rightful and proper time, we dipped our fingers into the clay, turned sticks into brushes, and recorded our presence. Good old Energy was there all the time, ready and waiting to do its job, but until we made our appearance, repetition and humdrumness were the order of the day. Energy, powerful, indestructible and indefinable, is hidden until an intermediary becomes its agent. Minerals, vegetables, animals, people – little children – all are needed to prove Energy's existence and convey its power, for it is unknown and without influence until physical matter is put to work (or, perhaps, Energy calls it into being). If our children question their own significance, let them imagine what the world – or, for that matter, existence – would be like without them. Energy-infused intellect is mandatory.

A trip to the forest preserve will be a special day; all children love nature. 'Look, there, see the minnows?' 'Hey, Wal-Hum, watch the frog jump!' The children will take notes and list all the different life forms they find, and the next day everyone will pass the quiz with flying colours because the outing was such fun. But there is a wonderful lesson hidden in the forest retreat. Becoming acquainted with the pollywog, and the pond with its whirling teeming life, can be a window to understanding. Sitting up straight and thinking thoughts, the children will enjoy the arithmetical riddle of the lily pond:

A lily pad is placed in a pond. Each day thereafter, the pad and all of its descendants double. On the 30th day the pond is covered completely with lily pads, which can grow no more. On which day was the pond half full and half empty? The 29th day.

When the children begin to think creatively, they will tap into the flow and find hidden meanings. In this instance, it will be easy for the children to foresee their own future when they envision their own environments hanging in the balance, overpopulated or dysfunctional in any way.

Back in the classroom, the children will compare notes and share their discoveries. They will listen to Wal-Hum's report (he was the brave one who caught the pollywog in his cupped hands). 'It was so beautiful! So perfect, and I could just *feel* its Energy. I thought of bringing it back to school, but then I realized that it was *more perfect* at home in the pond.' Wal-Hum learned a great deal at the outing.

Considerations such as these will help our children understand that physical matter is the costume that Energy wears in order to display its power – with and through endless particularity. This knowledge will also give our children the awareness that diversity is normal and natural and necessary, and that their special allotment of this life-giving force is what makes them what they are. If our children were all the same, their particles dipped from the same *mélange*, they would reflect the same interminably boring, irksome, monotonous uniformity. As it is, however, each of our children is a prize waiting to be opened.

****

What may the consequences be if we fail to share the evidences of this secret realm? Well, first of all, we should not be surprised if the children perceive their lives to be insignificant – even that it is pointless to survive in a meaningless world. And close to follow will be boredom and apathy, for many children find learning by rote, through fixed routines, without thought or understanding, to be inconsequential. To really understand, David must call on as many of his tools for learning (his senses) as he can. To truly learn about pyramids, David must read and think and dream about pyramids; he must travel across the ocean, climb up on a camel, find Cairo along the bank of the Nile, and then ***look*** and ***see*** the ancient tomb. He will ***touch*** and ***feel*** its massiveness, and he will ***listen*** to the silence and ***hear***, in his own far distant past, the cries of the million slaves who built it. He will breathe the air they breathed and he will ***taste*** the bitter fruit of their labour. Then David will know pyramids.

What will be the consequence when we share this secret?

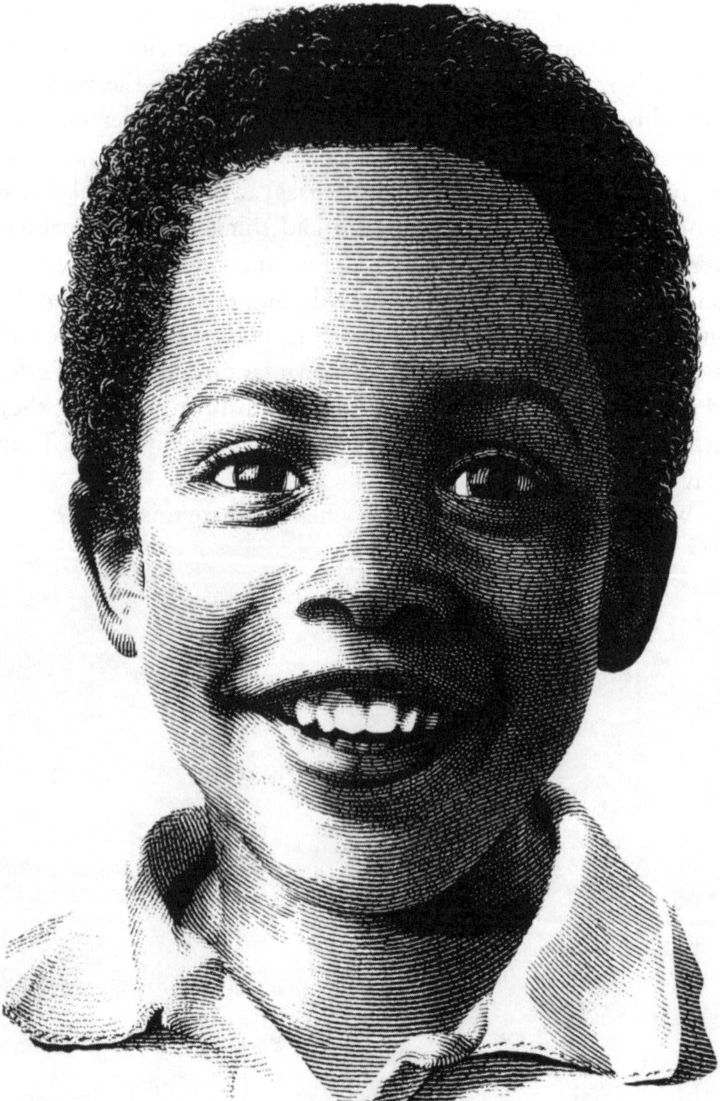

David

Knowledge and Understanding

Education does not mean teaching people to know what they do not know. It means teaching them to behave as they do not behave . . . It is not teaching the youth . . . the shapes of letters and the tricks of numbers; and then leaving them to turn their arithmetic to roguery, and their literature to lust. It is, on the contrary, training them into the perfect exercise and kingly continence of their bodies and souls. It is a painful, continual and difficult work; to be done by kindness, by watching, by warning, by precept, and by praise – but above all, by example.

John Ruskin (1866)[1]

In a sense, everything is a half, and to know its whole we must become acquainted with its partner. Ask the children to define a 'line'. They might start by describing what a line is not. It is not a dot (the line's alter ego). What is a straight line? A straight line is hard to define without knowing its counterpart – a crooked one. Rough needs smooth to find its identity. Light and dark, high and low, open and closed, alive and dead, female and male, smile and scowl – our children, making a game of it, will find the list a long one. And this equation relates to the non-physical, abstract world as well. Happiness is the other half of sadness. Love and hate, greed and generosity – hope, trust, desire, devotion, belief, truth – all have their opposites.

Such an exercise will help the children understand that their daily encounters will touch on both the material and non-material aspects of their lives. Going to school, mastering the magic of letters and numbers, will comprise much of their education. Learning the principles of mathematics, the theories of science, and the facts of history will train minds to store information and draw from its resources, but the deeper meanings toward which and for which this wealth of knowledge might lead will probably not be touched on. It is true that the proper use of words and all the facts and the figures will help our students fit into the waiting world, for these are essential tools, but facts alone can be irksome and tedious. They will not be fulfilling or bring happiness or self-confidence unless *purpose* and *meaning* are incorporated, and this bounty will remain hidden if we, as educators, do not share the secret of the existence of the hidden world of abstraction.

As our children become acquainted with the tools for learning, a process that has its beginnings in their earliest formative months and years, they will, from the outset, if carefully taught, gradually direct their Energy to serve *meaningful* goals. And the goals must be *appropriate* goals. Personal aggrandizement can lead to feelings of self-sufficiency, and thus the door is opened to isolation. This is the more serious and troublesome consequence, for this kind of behaviour is self-destructive, and our children can easily set themselves adrift.

Education is more than the acquisition of knowledge. The purpose of education is to prepare the individual to be a participant. Aptitudes, synchronized to the common good, find accordance and harmony in a function greater than their own. We can imagine the consequences when each individual participates in the manifestation of universal goals.

What we do with the tools of learning is the indeterminate factor, for our particularized focusing of Energy can give birth to wonderful achievements, or result in the infliction of horrendous despair. In our formative months, when we are just little tikes, we begin to reflect the influence of our surroundings and guidance, and when we enter the classroom some sixty or seventy months later, our dispositions and attitudes are already quite well defined.

Fitting into the spectrum of life – becoming a part of the social order, not only the human social order, but also the natural conformity presented in the surrounding environments and systems – is obligatory. In our human realm, the stability and integrity of every social structure – family, town, state and nation, even inter-nation – is qualified by the participation of each individual constituent. Since children are tomorrow's adults, they must find their assigned place in the scheme of things as quickly as possible, for the overall organization of life will ultimately undoubtedly reflect their participation, or their lack of participation.

****

Listening to the evening news, we cannot assimilate all the deprivation and unhappiness that flows over us like a heavy wave. It is unbecoming that we, the human beings, surrounded by beauty and majesty, should be contrary and dysfunctional – out of tune and worlds away. And this domain is waiting for the newborn babe. If this little one acquires the tools for learning and then surrenders them to egocentric goals, our kingdom's Energy will again be compromised, the waste will be confirmed, and the evening news will remain the same. We parents and teachers – parents as teachers – can help our children find their place and purpose by allowing the early introduction and exercise of imagination, investigation, and contemplation to come into their lives. We will be successful, because we are working with minds that are still untouched by misapplication.

However, the adult community, apparently without a sense of connection, is giving mixed signals to our young people through its outward admonitions and its inward coalition with dishonesty, indifference and greed. Through advertising and other forms of commercialism, we deliberately mislead. Violence and anger and inanity are presented and acknowledged as entertainment: the little child deserves better. Subservience to debilitating substances, hateful, even indolent, behaviour, and vain and nullifying thought disrupt Energy's natural flow, and the consequences are grist to the media's mill. When the torment becomes intolerable we strengthen law enforcement, clamping down on the offenders, but what are we doing now about the kinds of abuses that targeted the embittered perpetrators when *they* were youngsters of tender age? It is obvious that the damage they now inflict was earlier directed at them. At such a time as this, when dysfunctionality so grievously inflicts its toll, we must be insistent and courageous as we, the teachers, call upon first principles. We must redefine education for our children.

Diversity

Disparity and diversity should be farther apart in our dictionaries. We might say that diversity is the plus side of disparity for it gives 'difference' a happy twist. In today's classrooms, children are called upon to measure up to predetermined and impersonal standards of excellence. We continue to approve the pyramid structure where the "best" is at the top, and the rest are assembled in diminishing degrees of importance below. If we subscribe to the premise that each child's capacities and aptitudes are unique – principally because of the manner and degree in which Energy manifests itself – then we must review the wisdom of competition in the schools.

Parents and teachers are keenly aware of the anguish a child suffers when his or her capacities, designed for particularity, are directed toward conformity. Is it little wonder that a child may shy away from initiative and individuality when these attributes are perceived in a negative light? We know that diversity makes the garden beautiful.

Within life's grand display, diversity is a normal attribute. All 110 elements comprising the mineral realm intermingle and correlate endlessly. The capacities of the lower kingdoms are fixed and captive in the mix. They are not able to step out of line and go their own way. Thankfully, young children (and old children) *can* step out of line and make life meaningful. Diversity is our most precious attribute. We must encourage the children to stand proud, make waves, contribute, and be noticed.

Oh, oh, Hamid has his hand up again: 'If I am made up of specific atoms of Energy, and these particles allow my individuality to present itself, *who* or *what* am "I" – the "Hamid" part? And all my friends – who are they? and all the people everywhere – surely they are more than clever bits of matter walking around and doing things!'

What is Hamid doing with his questioning? He is practising independent investigation. Throughout his life, as he examines and ponders, the spark of insight will accompany him – so long as he continues to 'ask those questions'! He will understand that to accept as truth the word of *any other person*, learned or not, will automatically deprive him of that truth – merely because he accepts it without understanding. This knowledge, in itself, will light up his world. These secrets, waiting for the inquiring mind, are less than a step away; they can click into consciousness and thought instantly, unannounced. When the children's Energy is so focused, purpose will come into their lives. It is here, in this private world, that *thinking* gives birth to *meaning*. Hamid will put on his thinking cap and ask questions his parents would not have thought to ask. 'Since all the various life forms employ Energy to show off their attributes, and as Energy is essential and universal, then are not all life forms parts of a wonderful oneness? Because "our" essence is the same, are we not all shareholders? Golly, could it be that I am truly connected with the universe – minerals, plants, animals and all?'

Consequences

When conceived in the womb, every child of the next generation is a miracle waiting to be born, and when born into the physical world, this bundle of Energy is ready to be opened. At the enigmatic moment of conception, when the father and mother's components meet and merge, a combination of elements that has never existed before allows unknowable potentialities to come into being. The relationship of each particle to particle, molecule to molecule and gene to gene – held secret in this newly formed infant – will enable Energy to be manifested throughout its life in wondrous but nonetheless restricted and particularized ways. After all, as tiny tots we know nothing by ourselves, and we will know only what we are taught. Oh, as youngsters, we may become aware of simple consequences: touch something hot – we won't do that again; nursing a bruised knee or scraped elbow – stay on top of the roller blades. If we take the largest piece of cake, and are not advised, we will naturally expect to have the biggest and best as our due. Why? Why not?

From the beginning, the newborn infant is sheltered and nourished, and gradually learns the guidelines that will progressively enable it to function on its own. Most of these lessons have to do with consequences.

Youngsters learn bit by bit that if they do or say 'this', then they can expect 'that' to happen. Even our very little ones can anticipate the effect of a cause. 'What will happen if I take the largest piece of cake?' 'If I talk back to the teacher or my parents, what might happen?'

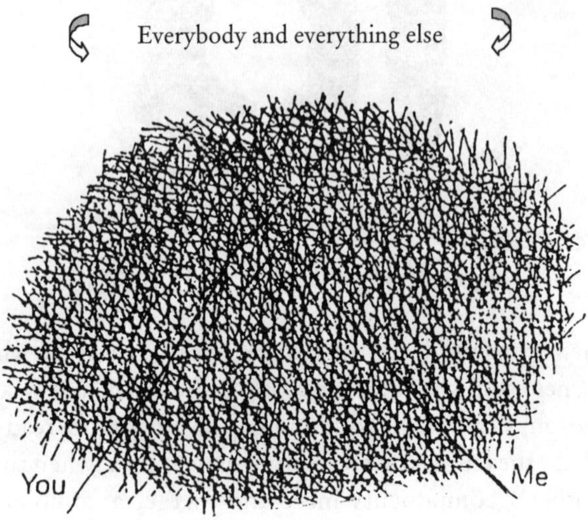

Consequences

When we are born, all that we can claim to possess is potential. Then, as the days pass, every great and small event that presents itself is a consequence that must be attended to. We are constantly reacting to initiatives that have had their beginnings either close by or far away. And it is reciprocal, for what *we* do and what *we* say ultimately affects others with whom we have no direct contact; the chains of causes and effects go out in all directions.

The students may enjoy the following story. Two women are shopping at the mall. As they pass the jewellery section, one of them pauses, turns to her friend and asks:

'Did you ever receive a gift that was the most precious and most treasured gift of all, and do you remember who gave it to you?'

Her friend thinks for a moment and then replies, 'Yes, I do remember such a gift, and, yes, I remember who gave it to me. It was given to me by my parents.'

'What was the gift?'

'Well, it was my life. My parents gave me my life.'

The children may transfer this story to their own lives and ask themselves, 'What about *my* parents . . . and my grandparents? And what about my grandparents' grandparents, and on and on way back in history? What part did those early people play in my being here now? Do we thank them too?' And the discussion might take a turn: 'What about all the *things* that have happened to me since I was born? Every sight that I saw, every sound I heard, every taste and smell and touch – did each increment make me what I am? Am I the sum of all these circumstances? If so, I had best be careful about my judgement of others, for I cannot know what consequences have shaped their lives up to the moment of our meeting.'

Education and Competition

Victory breeds hatred, for the conquered is unhappy.
Gautama Buddha[2]

Every age and time reflects the degree of Energy that can be made known in it. Every physical form enrolled in the mineral, vegetable, animal or human kingdoms shares in this endeavour. At one time our world was a silent sphere, dormant but infused with unknowable promise. Like a seed, waiting for the spring season, fruition bided its time. Today, after eons of incubation, our planet blossoms and life abounds.

The challenge that life presents is one of survival. Sustaining the equilibrium in any organism depends on the relationship of its integral parts to the function of the whole. Our world, before we came on the scene, evolved with incredible conformity – incredible indeed, for all life's forms interacted perfectly (well, ate each other) and balance was maintained. Then, after some long time, we knocked at the door, the door opened and we entered the fray.

In olden times, when our ancestors were struggling to survive (even more than we are today), being distanced from each other offered some degree of security. The intrusion of another family, looking favourably at some nearby real estate, would have been a cause of considerable concern; Neanderthal housing projects were few and far between, and the accommodation a new family might be looking at, no matter how far away, was not far enough. If I had been one of those early people, tending the fire at the mouth of our cave, I'm sure my watchful eye would have been scanning the horizon, on the lookout. And if man or beast were to come into view, I would have grabbed my club (if I could have found it) and headed over there to tell the newcomers to get lost. When the burly fellow in charge saw me approaching, obviously not on a mission to borrow a pinch of salt for my woman's culinary venture, we two he-men, with hardly a grumble, would vie for position and commence to set to it to set things right.

****

Apparently such behaviour sticks with you when you learn it in an early age.

Over the centuries the blows have become less direct and more remotely delivered. The point of the weapon has extended further from the hand that brandishes it. From flint knife to axe to spear, from arrow to gunshot and missile to threatening to press the button, today the domination of an individual (or a nation) over another continues. We teach our children to be competitive, to measure their own capacities and accomplishments against the performance of others.

This idea presents a very different set of rules from the ones that ideally define the structure of the family where everyone is to consider as beyond reproach the innate capacities of everyone else. When they leave home and enter the classroom, how are our youngsters to reason that the one coveted prize belongs to the 'winner' when they, the 'contestants', are competing with varying and unequal capabilities? Of course the fastest runner will win the race, and the keenest mind will score the scholastic victory. A single standard, by which different and particularized capacities are to be measured, is a perplexing concept.

We have neglected to inform our children that an individual life is precious, and that mysteries are hidden within. We have kept secret the quest: that the material world is the matrix Spirit uses to manifest its presence and achieve its goal.

The observation here presented argues that we are neglecting to inform our children that life is more than it appears to be. Physical existence has the upper hand, for everything seems to have a substantial presence. It is not surprising if the children perceive themselves to be only corporeal. From the outset, advertising and other forms of commercialism present a lopsided view of what lies ahead. As parents and teachers, we support this impression by directing schoolchildren's attention to the physical aspects of their journey. Learning the lessons, finding a career, raising a family, saving for retirement, securing funds for the funeral, where is the excitement? Where do the hopes and dreams fit in? When and where, in the present curriculum, does the thrill of discovery make its appearance? In the humdrumness of our teaching we have left out the romance. We are unduly cautious in protecting our children; we blink, look evasively at the meaningful aspects of life, because there is taint associated with matters other than factual matters. This yielding implies disquietude or (hopefully not) indifference. In our vigilance to protect our children's freedom, it is difficult to understand the sanctions we have imposed on their freedom to experience the value and significance of creative thinking.

****

It is here proposed that the school curriculum include a time period devoted to rational thought and independent investigation. It would accompany the students from the first grade on up. The youngest children would be taught the principles of 'consequence', and through this knowledge they would gradually understand that things do not just happen, but are brought about by a cause. All kinds of subjects could be incorporated in the discussion. 'What might happen if I took the biggest piece of cake at Mary's party? Well, the other kids wouldn't like it; they would think I was being greedy.' Or, 'If my mother heard about it, she would be disappointed.'

Later on, other leading questions might come to mind: How do people living in very difficult geographical environments survive? Why did some cultures develop technology, and others did not discover the wheel? Rosa might ask, 'In the structure of the family, what part does "sacrifice" play in its functioning; what do parents and children have to "give up" to be participants? And is there a comparison that would apply in the relationship of nation to nation?' And Kara: 'Could competition and the importance of winning, say, in sports, support the idea that for boys to become men they must be aggressive and dominate? And might this learned behaviour lead to all the fighting inside and outside the home later on?' And Sylvie: 'Why did religion play so important a role in people's lives that civilizations were named after them? And, how did arithmetic come into being?'

The subject matter is not as important as the speculations that might be induced. This approach to teaching would bring into context the physical factors (memorizing and remembering), and the non-physical aspects (thinking and processing and applying) that enable such knowledge to be meaningful. When we inform the children that the factual material, and the abstract use of this material, are the two parts of education, they will understand the importance of all those facts and figures.

It is suggested that there be no right or wrong answers, no papers to hand in – unless someone is so excited about his or her discovery that copies will be handed out to the other students. The children would, perhaps take notes. Then, when Elizabeth poses her question, 'I know when I feel sick, but what part of me is sad?' her classmates will add this question to their stockpile and perhaps, some day, independently find the answer.

From Atom to Art

We do not normally consider what we do as art. Those of us who are lawyers or chemists, sales managers, bankers or bricklayers, may be of the opinion that art is a gift bestowed on painters or poets or musicians and we, the common folk, feeling perhaps disadvantaged, are left outside. If someone mentions that he or she is an artist or musician, predictable responses are triggered: 'How wonderful! Me, I can't draw a straight line,' or, 'I can't carry a tune in a basket.'

Most of us start our journey with no particular agenda. We play soccer with friends at school or plan some back-yard adventure, but few of us, in our early years, find a compelling interest in, say, playing the piano. We are, for the most part, quite passive; unmindful of the learning process that is quietly at work. Unaware of the influence of countless twists of fate, we gradually, perhaps unwittingly, find interests and aptitudes that are hidden within, and it is then that our lives become meaningful. Secretly, we are tapping into the flow.

But the 'we' part is the puzzling part, for we are more than the effects we make happen. Some of us are musicians, but what are we, the ones behind the music? (This was Hamid's question.) What might we call ourselves – we who aspire to foresee and then direct eyes and ears and hands to make the dream real? We *mentally* conceive, then *physically* give birth to the vision so that our intent can be, with wonder, acknowledged.

We make music, and what might the music (the effect) call us other than its maker (cause)? And as such, might we not consider ourselves, as well, the effect of a cause that cannot be fathomed? Although what we are is a mystery, what this mystery does is real and true. Our physical make-up, configurations composed of smatterings of those 110 elements (arranged as enabling molecules) serve us as tools. Voices, ears, eyes, hands and feet – look at us go!

Baking a wonderful pie is not what it seems. It is actually a mystical happening! The pie itself is a puzzle; why should such a conglomeration of atoms taste so good? But more remarkable is the chain of causes and effects bringing it to its place on the County Fair Home Arts table. Look at the variety, and don't they all look delicious? Over there we can see the contestants standing off to one side anxiously waiting for the judges to make their decision. If we listen carefully we can hear the pie-lady in the blue sweater: 'Well, it looks to me like Ada's pie is going to win again.' To you and me, Ada's pie looks pretty much like all the others, but those who know pies will be able to affix the blue ribbon to the best one. It's a 'spiritual' thing. Ada and her pie somehow validate and entitle each other – Ada makes the pie, and what does the pie do? The pie makes Ada a pie-maker.

Another scenario: Back around the turn of the century, Nashville, Indiana (Barbara's and my hometown), was a small country village nestled in the hills of Brown County. Washboardy roads paved the way. We can picture Jake's wagon shop situated a quarter mile east of the centre of things. A typical hot summer day, flies are buzzing, and Jake and his cronies are idly talking, not much going on. A man approaches toting a broken wheel, the rim is bent and several spokes are missing. No one says anything, but they all study the wheel. Jake finally says, 'Well, this is a job for Jim,' and he turns his head and calls over his shoulder to the back of the shop, 'Hey, Jim, come on out here.' Jim stands quietly, pondering the wheel, arms sort of folded, one hand at his chin, and he says, 'Yeah, I can do that.' Well, why can Jim fix the wheel and the others cannot? It is because Jim and his work are one. Jim gets out of the way, the Energy flows through, and the wheel is fixed.

And one more: How many times has a gallery guard, watching the masterpieces in the Louvre, heard whispered, 'Oh! Look at Cézanne!' 'That's Van Gogh!' Well, yes, they *are* wonderful, but they *are* dead. However, what they did when they were alive was to so put themselves into their work that their signatures are not necessary. Like Ada's wonderful pie, the paintings identify their makers.

All these interesting people are Energy channellers, and what they do is the consequence of how they are put together – how their atoms and molecules are so arranged and synchronized as to allow Energy to express itself in such particular and marvellous ways.

A pie-maker may be a pie-maker and an artist may be an artist, but without producing a masterpiece, who would know? Without the evidences displayed, Ada, Cézanne, and Jim the wheelwright would join the ranks of undistinguished common folk. This lesson is directed to our children. If they quietly sit in the corner, watching TV or clicking at their computer games, *they will not be noticed*.

It may be reasoned that life displays Energy in specific and measured degrees, enabling distinct and definable attributes to be known, *but what is Energy*, and where does it abide? Certainly the atoms and molecules are not in control of their own destiny (for they cannot know if they are being called upon to shape a rock or form a thought). And certainly *purpose* is involved, for all definable systems fit together in such a way that order, rather than chaos, is maintained, and a degree of completeness greater than their own is manifested. And, we can hardly avoid the question, called upon by what or whom? There are few options; the conclusion we arrive at must be stated something like this: Some universal enabling factor is at work controlling the constrained capacities of physical matter.

****

This discussion brings us to the place of art in our lives, particularly in the lives of our children. Not art as it is taught through lessons concerning composition and colour, but more importantly art as a *natural* fruition of human initiative and creativity – art as an evocation. When Energy flows through us, art is born. The alerted mind conceives, then calls upon the intermediate tools – and what happens? Prizewinning pies and fixed wheels come into existence.

Little children are fundamentally innocent. They are not inherently instilled with knowledge; it is an acquired attribute that must be learned. In our schools, numbers and letters are taken care of quite satisfactorily, but the children are not told, and they do not know, that there is another side to the knowledge equation. They are unaware that they are luminaries, each one holding the torch of progress, which when held high will light up the world.

****

We have another challenge. Attaching definitive significance to the lessons and assignments by which knowledge is acquired is of little consequence. Mathematics, social studies, language arts and physical science are the *means*, the intermediate tools for learning, but they are meaningless if they fail to facilitate understanding and perception. The children are unaware that wondrous *non-physical* aptitudes and talents are hidden within their *physical* substance – unique capabilities instilled when they were conceived, endowments waiting to be set free – each and every one an art form. Tragically, these will remain unrealized, a mere potential, if the children are not informed of what it is that they are – and how the lessons and assignments will ultimately enable them to touch on meaning and purpose. When they 'step aside', let Energy flow through naturally and freely, they will become wellsprings of progress. Channelling their Energy, they will establish the culture of their time.

The Mischief-maker

At this point, I would like to tell one of my father's stories. As I recall, he would begin by saying, 'This is a Turkish story.'

Long ago and far away there was an owner of a great estate. The barns and pastures and the hills beyond were his, as was the wonderful mansion nearby. One would think things were going well for a man in his position, but he was troubled; the daily chores were without end and try as he might, he could not find enough servants to help. One day while he was working in his garden, worrying about his plight, he looked up to see a young man coming up the path. He looked strong and amiable; his stride was brisk and he was smiling as he approached.

They exchanged greetings and the traveller asked if he might see the owner of the estate, as he was looking for work. The owner replied that he was the master, and, 'Yes, how wonderful that you should come by at such a time when I have so great a need. I can put you to work right away. What terms might we agree upon?'

The young man replied that there were two stipulations, and that both must be complied with. One was that he must be kept busy, and the other was that he was not to be paid a wage. The owner was puzzled, but he agreed and they clasped hands closing the deal.

The estate owner thought and planned for a moment and then told the young man to start his chores by cleaning the stables and barns. The fellow set off with a lively step and the gardener returned to his plantings, musing on his good fortune. Just a few minutes had passed when he looked up and there was this smiling fellow asking what his next job should be, the barns are clean. The owner was taken aback and went to inspect the work. It was better than he had hoped for. He was perplexed, but he turned to the young man and told him to fetch water and feed for the cattle, and then groom the horses. And off the fellow went humming a tune.

A short time later he returned; all the work had been done, and he asked for his next assignment. This state of affairs continued on into the afternoon and when the fellow returned from his last task, the gardener was confused and undecided and told him: 'Sit over there and wait a minute; let me think.' The young man said that this would not do; the agreement was that he must be kept busy. Desperate, the owner instructed him to move the far hill to the east side of the estate; the drainage would be better and the view from the manor house would be more beautiful.

The worker headed for the hills with shovel in hand, but was back within the hour; the work was finished. The owner now was deeply troubled and said that he needed a moment to decide what other work needed to be done. 'Sit and rest while I consider.' Dejected, the young man turned away, and, after a moment, the gardener heard an uproar – shouting and yelling. Looking up, he saw one of his barns on fire. Frantically, he ran to the scene and there, inside the barn, this young fellow was busy setting another fire. 'Here! Stop that!

Run and get water and call for others to come and help.' The young man immediately dropped his torch, sounded the alarm, and rushed to the pumps for water.

In the midst of all this confusion, another traveller approached the landowner. He was very aged but his eyes were bright and his countenance betokened great wisdom. 'Well, stranger, it looks like you have got yourself into a bit of trouble.' The owner then related the story of the young man's arrival and the problems that had ensued. The old man replied, 'You don't know who this young man is, do you?' The estate owner replied that he thought he was just a fellow looking for work. The wise one said, 'Let me explain, but first, as the fires are almost out, call him over here. I will tell him what to do and your problems will be over.' The amiable young man approached and the old traveller told him: 'Go over to that pole and climb up and down until your master tells you to stop.' The fellow rushed over to the pole and started climbing.

'Now, let me tell you who this young man is. He is called the mind, and the pole is his hobby. Unless the mind is kept busy, it creates mischief.'

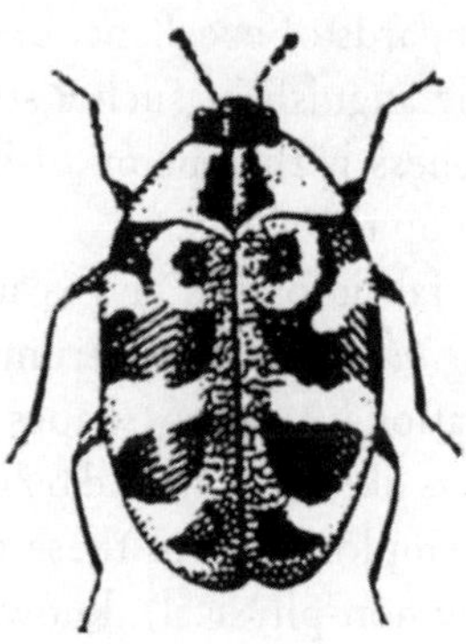

The child in the womb has not asked to be there, nor is the newly conceived one free to choose the bestowals that are to define and oversee its journey.

Does it not seem unfair that this little one, untouched and pure, designed for particularity and gifted with unknowable promise, should be enrolled in a competitive world where predetermined and impersonal standards of excellence are to measure its worth? Can we imagine the anguish of such a soul? Conformity stifles initiative, and sameness is the enemy of diversity, the wondrous attribute that lights up the world.

Diversity is the fabric of life and is inherent in all systems, *tangible and intangible*. Life's spectrum not only reflects all knowable configurations, colours, shapes and sizes, bur, as well, the indefinable things like thought and behaviour, compassion and love. Through the employment of these two fundamentals (i.e., the physical and the non-physical), knowledge is enhanced with understanding. It is then that the child will find *meaning* hidden within the incredible display and, though difficult to define, he will acknowledge it as real and true.

Ideas themselves are mystifying; they come into being unannounced, without our beckoning. Sitting quietly, perhaps reading or watching TV or drying the dishes, suddenly we are changed, different from what we were before the interlude. Some inexplicable transformation has taken place and we look at things in a new light. The revelation is so momentous that we realize we will never be the same, and we cannot but wonder from whence such insights come?

But some ideas do identify their beginnings. The principles outlined here are easily traced to their source. It would be unfair to claim them as my own, for they embrace a universal perspective that is beyond my field of vision. These principles, proclaimed by Bahá'u'lláh, and exemplified by His son 'Abdu'l-Bahá, bring into context the two polarities of science and religion, points of view that have troubled us for so long. 'Abdu'l-Bahá's discourses and writings clearly define the reciprocal relationship of the physical and the more-than-physical aspects of existence. With simple but profound explanations, a theory of evolution is clearly defined, and the proposition that *cause* and *effect* are inherent in every facet of life cannot but be acknowledged.

Yes, ideas are wonderful, but these are special because they address the fundamental needs of a divided world. Old concepts, coveted for their past service, now stunt our growth. Our great need is to find a common discipline that will align our Energy to a single purpose and then hold us to the line. As we cannot explain the phenomena of fresh concepts infusing and alerting our thoughts, we must concede that their disclosure comes *through us* from an Energy source beyond all reason. So, let's give revelation a round of applause, for it ultimately enables us to find our way.

Today, our scientists are busier than ever before, delving into the materiality of life in their attempts to find the 'unified field' behind everything. Every so often they share their excitement; they are 'getting closer', but then the answers seem to slip away, retreating further and deeper into complex intangibles. And religion, content to relegate the mysteries of life to the province of an unknowable omnipotence, continues to hold fast to practices that increasingly dissipate the indivisible Energy that connects us to the greater realm. These two schools may be satisfactory for their followers, but what about the rest of us who are bothered when their two truths are in contention with each other?

History records that, apparently, a determined allotment of knowledge is made available for our use at any particular time. We cannot step ahead of the game. Throughout the ages, great thinkers discover new, timely, and often outlandish ideas that change or replace the old outmoded ones. Their dreams, however fanciful at the time, become manifest, and in due course are instrumental in furthering our progress. In earlier times, superstition and dogma clouded our vision, but when science came on the scene, with its reliance on reasonable proof, our understanding of the workings of life changed completely. Now it is clear that the physical presentation cannot be known other than by and through its non-physical attributes. In one sense, we *are* ahead of the game for (because of science) we are privy to a perception which science itself is, for the most part, still reluctant to explore. We must thank the biochemists and genetic researchers for helping us touch on the mystery of life's dual nature, for we common folk could never have found the mystery by ourselves.

At this point, my argument would appear to have little to do with religion, but carrying it a bit further we must concede that advancement, the movement forward toward specific goals, is reflected by all systems, mankind included. The employment of abstract thought has exerted so great an influence on our progress that civilizations have been named after the religions that gave them birth. From cave to nation, the structure of the social order has built on principles that have focused the Energy of diverse peoples on the achievement of a unified progress. Expanded understanding has resulted in new and advanced technology and art. It is interesting, but perhaps not surprising, that religion, using the logic of science, should in this day lead the way and construct the bridge connecting the two worlds.

The two courses of study that will help our children fit into this, their era of enlightenment, are, it is here proposed, *independent investigation of truth* (through the asking of questions and the assessment of answers), and *an understanding of the oneness of the physical and non-physical aspects of life.* Then, when Elizabeth and David face the challenge of a new and reasonable premise, former perceptions will change or be enhanced and they will see more clearly. They will, with intent, become participants in the evolutionary process.

This proposal does not entail the building of new schools. It changes the perspective, redefines the goals that public education aspires to achieve. It is a gift that we can, with great love, share with our children. We will teach the facts and figures; they will use these tools to find meaning and purpose and everything, *everything*, will change.

PART TWO

SPIRIT MATTERS

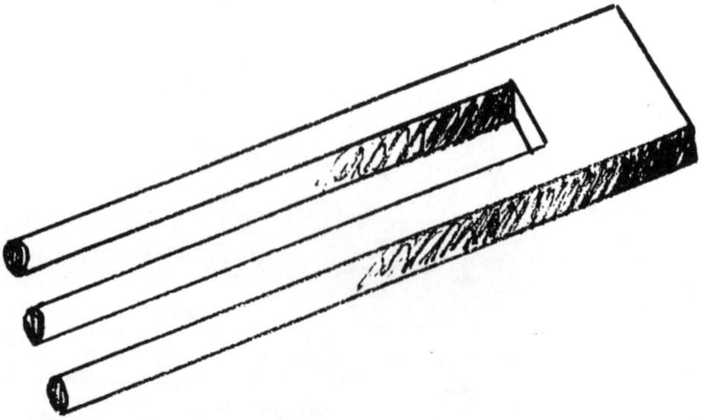

Sometimes things appear to be possible, but there is something amiss.

And sometimes things are possible, but appear not to be.

The Mobius Strip

This perplexing strip of paper has just one side, and one edge.

We human beings are programmed to accept concepts that prove to be true, and our intellect allows us to reject ideas that do not fall in line. But sometimes we are called upon to acknowledge, as true, considerations that cannot be proven, but do fall in line.

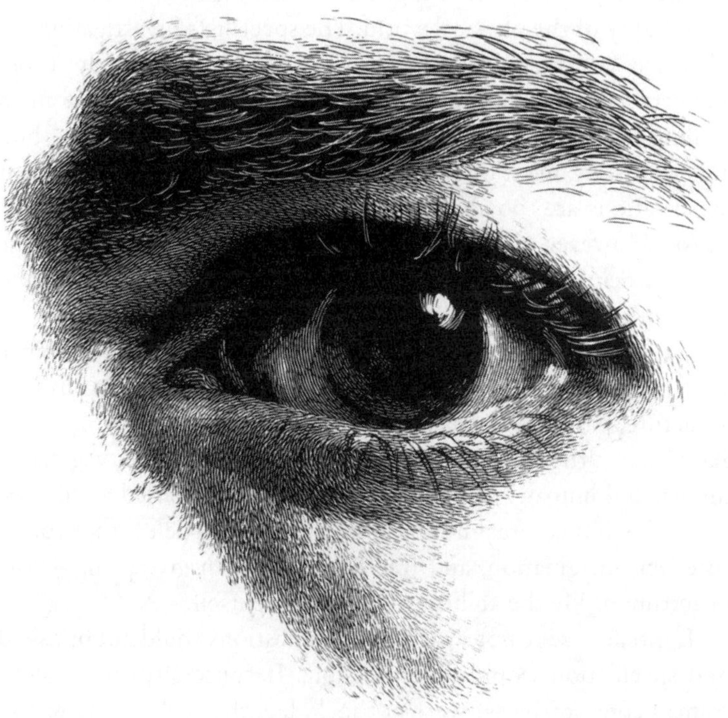

INSIGHT

When we speak of the universe, we are attempting to describe in mere words all the complexities of existence; that in this special all-inclusiveness we cannot conceive of anything that might have been left out. We, the ones who can speculate about such matters, are in size somewhere midway between the atoms that compose us and the stellar galaxies that surround us.

We all agree that the essential nature of existence is beyond comprehension. But, what about the *identity* of existence, the designation of its attributes; is this closed off to us as well?

Science in general, with its logic, is unrelenting in its search for the materiality of the physical world. The specialists investigating the abstruse complexities of particle physics, particularly those concerned with the double-helix chains of the DNA, are most willing to impart their findings to the outside world, but, unfortunately, most of us common folk can only acquiesce; their explanations are too abstruse for our general knowledge to fully grasp. However, the depth of their inquiries does not alter the basic principles on which they are based, and we all can understand the fundamentals.

We know that the atom is the key entity that enables existence to express itself. It participates in the formation of every physical structure, past, present, and future, known and unknown. As we have seen, although the different kingdoms – mineral, vegetable, animal and human – may manifest specific and varied attributes, only the human realm can utilize these particles to express intellect, imagination, and free will, therewith giving the whole spectrum of life the ability to contemplate itself.

If intellect were not a part of it all, questions could not be asked and speculation would be impossible. If consciousness (that is, human consciousness) were not included, the cycle of life would course through its sequences without significance; plants would grow and animals would roam, but evolution and repetition would remain a well-kept secret. For the processes of life to be justified, a capacity that can comprehend its organization and its function must be incorporated as well.

But even if we are here to witness the spectacle and analyse the mysteries, what actually is accomplished? Is our awareness reason enough for the whole display? Yes, we think and we search for meaning, but why must there be meaning? Is it not plausible that the entire complexity run through its routines, evoking nothing of *real* consequence and designed for no particular purpose at all? Watching, as best we can, the workings of life, this might be a logical, though depressing, conclusion if several discernible signs were not in evidence.

- The first is borrowed from the patterns and disciplines that describe what we call the evolution of life. What is happening in the maturing of each plant and animal and human being, and what is taking place in the evolution of its parent species, gives evidence of a basic plan to which all aspects relate. The entire process describes a chain of causes and effects bringing forth one condition from another, and this motion implies a fulfilment of purpose. If life presents evidence of a basic function in one phase of its structure, we must assume this verity runs through all of its manifestations. Reason tells us the stone must embrace the capacities of the atom. The ocean cannot display properties that are not inherent in the raindrop.
- A second consideration, which supports existence as favoured with meaning, is the passive submissiveness of each living form to a compatibility greater than its own. That each has, in this regard, no will to find its own way attests to the presence of a universal intent for which each one is designed. The yielding of the parts to the function of the whole, whether the whole is an atom with its whirling electrons, the earth with its resident species, or the universe with its unnumbered systems, a oneness of purpose is implied. Rather than chaos, unity is manifested through diversity, and purpose is achieved.
- A third proposition necessitates, initially, the relatively easy assignment of the nature of material existence to a non-physical reality. The redefining of the forces that summon the varieties, the shapes and sizes, and that cause and regulate their essential non-physical properties will, it is suggested, reveal an Energy that instils particular purpose in all forms. When assembled, these organized parts fit together to reflect a universal integrity, and point to the existence of a creative cause bringing forth a purposeful effect.

These three patterns of thought are not meant to be merely interesting concepts, but are offered as important considerations in the development of a relevant course of inquiry for our young children. Helping them to find their place in the scheme of things, the importance of that place and the meaning of that place are, today, most relevant and desirable objectives.

Before we go further, however, let us agree on the meanings we want the words to convey. Throughout this discussion reference is made to the 'non-physical' nature of existence, to the 'spiritual' qualities that define the myriad shareholders of what we describe as creation. If you are not comfortable with these terms, please substitute your own (I like mine, but yours are probably better for you). We will be talking about the underlying meanings, about the *signs* that give evidence, and the *forces* that motivate, and the right words are hard to find.

But the nomenclature is not important. Whatever names or terms are used to designate this unknowable, abstract factor (that makes things 'work') will be satisfactory. 'Energy' is a good one (capitalized to designate its primacy), but what about 'Life' or 'Power' or my choice, 'Spirit'? Ask the children to make up a word, any word they like ('Zing might be good?') that would designate, for them, this undefined but essential constituent, which, as they mature, they will perceive to be fundamental to an understanding of the identity and meaning of their own lives.

The consideration of the physical world and its attributes will comprise much of our children's education. They will study about Energy and how all life depends on the exchange of this Energy for its existence. From atom to universe, every form manifests this indestructible 'force', and no matter how this force is used, or what form is using it, it is never lost. This truth, relating to the physical world, is an interesting branch of knowledge, but there is much more excitement hiding behind the scenery in the intangible world, and it is to the reality of this existence that our children shouldbe introduced.

But how are we to do this? Today, an inquiry into the non-physical nature of physical matter, if not perceived as mere speculation, may be viewed as an indoctrination of ideas infringing on childrens' rights. However, although our youngsters are working with the *mystery of occurrence*, the *display of phenomena*, every moment of their lives, they will not be able to articulate their feelings and attribute meaning to the evidences shown if they are unaware that such an existence exists.

Initially, this will be a strange way of looking at things, but as the children begin to think in these terms and with such a perspective, they will find they are closer to an understanding of the basics of life. Materiality and spirituality, those two embittered antagonists, will be revealed as two manifestations of the one truth. The children will gradually understand that their own area of function is not in the physical world at all, that their residence is in the spiritual realm where their hopes and dreams are born and abide. They live *within*. It is only when they speak or sing, paint, write or dance that they become apparent and the cause of an effect. If they do none of these things, they will not be noticed. As essentially non-physical beings in this physical environment, they need the physical tools, the vocal cords, paint and brush, and pencil and paper, and feet, to make their presence known.

As our young inquirers begin to direct their attention to the spiritual side of the equation, marvellous insights will be revealed. This is where they leave behind the factual data, the letters and numbers, and enter the world of meaningful abstraction. They all know that the rock is solid, the plant grows, the animal roams, and that the human being contemplates. But what is it that is responsible for this astonishing display? Why is the rock solid? What *compels* the flower to grow and the animal to roam? Good questions! And the children will no doubt ask, 'What are we, that we can imagine and think about things?' After all, physically (and, as we shall see, spiritually) everything is made up of the same components. What causes the same elemental particles to display such extraordinary and dissimilar behaviour?

Granted, these are not new questions, but today's children have sufficient information available to interpret the signs and give significance to the findings as never before. Their ancestors, the early peoples, having less information with which to work regarding the basic structures, the nature of the earth, water, and air – the solids, liquids, and gases – attributed the display to the presence of the supernatural, the workings of a force beyond human understanding. The argument offered here is based on this same premise, but is enhanced to support the concept that existence, in its entirety, its physical, *and* its non-physical attributes, is one reality. The physical composition of each life form, and the spiritual emanation that is evoked, are coexistent; the presence of the one necessitates the presence of the other. Hidden within this great oneness are great mysteries. One implies that the perfection and purpose of each individual part becomes fulfilled and more meaningful when its capacities are directed to the achievement of a function greater than its own (the leaf we hold in our hand is perfect, but was 'more perfect' when it was attached to the tree). Another implies that the integral parts cannot have independent or individual identity without having a connection to each other and to the whole (the identity of the bee is interwoven with its purpose, and it is only in its relationship to the hive and the honey that its purpose is realized). And the final point to be made is that the whole, from smallest to largest, from atom to universe, from leaf to tree, from human being to mankind, is defined and controlled by non-physical, spiritual laws (remember, you are using your own words). In their quest, our children will find such truths most helpful.

The division of creation into kingdoms and the assignment of each form to its appropriate residence will help our youngsters recognize the unified nature of existence. Rather than focusing on the differences that identify and separate the various forms, and what they might regard as the forms' independent functions, the children will gradually perceive a wonderful congruity and singleness of purpose with which all participants unwittingly comply. This will help them find their own place in this spectacular phantasmagoria. Our young inquirers will not find it difficult to understand the following hypothesis introduced earlier (p. 15):

Non-physical Energy activates everything. The pebble (atoms of iron, magnesium, phosphorus, silicon, etc.) holds together and assumes a shape because of the "spiritual power" we call ***cohesion***. A force, not inherent in the substance of the pebble's component minerals, gathers the elemental parts together and forms a structure. Atoms and molecules do not have a natural innate tendency to bond together. Some indefinable force from outside their own constitution instils in them an affinity that enables their parent mineral kingdom to present to the worlds of existence an endless variety of combinations, from asbestos to mercury, from a grain of sand to the stellar gases surrounding the most distant galaxy.

With the bonding of its atomic particles, the vegetable realm expresses life in the mineral degree, but the force we name ***growth*** has been directed to its substance as well. In consequence, and not by choice, the atoms collectively organize, respond to the warmth of the sun, embrace the nutrients of the soil, and bring forth the verdant sustenance of terrestrial life.

Sense perception and ***instinctual behaviour*** are some of the spiritual qualities identifying the animal realm and overseeing its substances. The universal atoms, comprising the structure (organs, tissues, and occasionally bones) of every living creature, are energized to roam, swim, or fly as Spirit puts them to work. The gnat and the hippopotamus are kindred spirits.

And we human beings, via the energy of Spirit, do not only have our atoms bundled together, nor do we merely develop from seed to seed, or expend our lives responding (it would seem more than less) to a prescribed animal discipline. Amidst all created forms, our manifested spiritual capacities allow us to think and choose. In our eagerness for knowledge, we search for truth. Throughout this terrestrial journey, ***reason*** is the faculty that enables us to "make the rounds" and find our way. It accompanies us wherever we go. We learn by thinking and choosing. But our substance also evokes such attributes as hope and faith, and these spiritual capacities give our lives meaning. With reason, ***hope***, and ***faith***, we set out on our

journey of discovery. If we are taught, we will value certitude. If we are instructed, we can develop a conscience that holds us to a purpose. Just think what our atoms enable us to do! We can love. We can laugh. (Who's laughing? are our atoms having a good time?) These spiritual attributes would forever be hidden were we not included in the representation of life. Without human awareness, existence would be the best-kept secret of all time.

However, a consideration of the identifying non-physical nature of the patterns and cycles that control the structure of life in general, and the children's lives in particular, is an aspect whose value is today seen as questionable. Introducing our children to the *meanings*, encouraging them to discover their own sensitivity to the wonders of awareness, is considered a hypothetical conjecture that must reside outside the regular classroom experience. Nonetheless, the awakening of the children's innate capacities to reflect and evaluate is certainly not accomplished merely by memorizing the facts and figures of the daily routine. Speculations, how wonderful! Considerations, most certainly! Our children's lives will always be made up of such intellectualization. What are the causes that lead to an effect? What are the factors that play a part and would the outcome be different if the input had been changed? If the children take part in the class play, or the concerns of the family, or if they do not, what might the consequences be? Even the very little ones will be able to take part in this exercise. If such considerations are not addressed *in the classroom*, the environment where questions originate and minds are set in motion, the children may develop unaware of the importance and meaning of their lives.

However, outlining for the children the obligation they have to themselves and to others to actively participate in the staging of life's spectacle is, today, not considered relevant to their educational and psychological needs. Although the mastering of common knowledge is a requisite for career achievement and certainly for the management of life's everyday happenstance, the *purpose* of each child's existence *may be much more significant*. The repercussions of our withholding this kind of inquiry are everywhere apparent. They are reflected not only in our youngsters' frustration with the material world, wherein and unfortunately through our own efforts they are firmly grounded and systematically programmed to set their sights, but these innocent children are encouraged, as well, to achieve their victories through the subjugation and humbling of others. This is the more serious consequence, for the children can actually become isolated.

In theory, we can imagine the damage to the worth and effectiveness of any individual caused by isolating it from any of the kingdoms. Its fundamental identity is interwoven with its purpose, and its purpose is incorporated in its involvement with others. When the children study a tree, they can understand the importance of each leaf to the entire community of leaves; that, if they take just one from its branch, even the smallest and most hidden one, all the others will have to work harder to compensate for the loss. It is obvious that a single leaf is without purpose unless it is related to the entire tree of leaves. And so it is with the children and their participation in the dazzling disclosure of life.

Accountability

The interdependence and interaction of things is indeed baffling. How the individual parts work together to support the function of the whole is a wonderfully perplexing question. The search to uncover the mysteries, why things work as they do, how the physical world can present so wondrous a display of colour, form, and function, has been the mission of countless seekers and the aim of endless speculation. And to propose that the answer to such questions is to be found in this little book is quite a proposal. But the agendas submitted by our two standards of judgement, science and religion, each questioning if not directly disputing the validity of the other, offer little assurance, so urgently needed, that a harmonious reconciliation is in the offing.

So far, for the most part our speculations have had exclusively either scientific or religious points of departure. Materiality and spirituality, the dual systems that define existence and embrace our kingdom in such manifest and bountiful ways, are not championed as one reality by either following. Our segregation of the *material* from the *spiritual*, assigning what we perceive as differences to opposing fields of study, is misleading our children. If truth is to be considered one – and it must – a fundamental precept validating both the material *and* the spiritual is absolutely essential.

The ultimate and inherent 'oneness of all things' demands that the integral parts, each and all, regardless of their aspect, be equivalent to the whole. The tiniest and simplest particle is as compelling as the largest and most complex one. This reasoning must include not only the material compositions that make up the overall physical presentation, but, as well, the laws that govern their form and function. The substances are one part of the equation, as are the disciplines that define their outward behaviour and innermost workings.

An awareness of the existence of these two factors must be made available to our young people. If we do not share the evidences of the cooperative relationship of the material and the non-material, the children will grow up with lop-sided knowledge. To learn about nature without being able to speculate about why all the myriad physical forms behave as they do is unfair, for it will formulate and establish patterns of thought that acknowledge only the material aspects of life. The inclusion and the necessity of the spiritual counterpart will remain secret and unknown.

My wife Barbara and I sit at our kitchen table watching the birds and the squirrels, keeping a sharp eye out for the deer back in the woods. The wonders of nature are displayed wherever we look, but our thoughts always bring us back to the problems we human beings are having, particularly in the larger cities where individuals, especially the children, become lost in the whirl of it all. Here the integrity of any of us could be in jeopardy, for the constraints that direct and control become insidious and all-consuming. This may not be true for all, but as the evening newscasters recount the events of the day it is evident that many of us, adults and children alike, are going through very difficult times.

Our problems are spiritual, although they are presented to us in perceptible and, often times, terrifying ways. Violence, anger, greed, and sensuality are the physical manifestations of our spiritual condition. We do not need to be antagonistic or selfish. With our free will our minds can direct our cerebral atoms to manifest love rather than hate, embrace generosity rather that greed. But this can happen only if our freedom to make these choices is disciplined by an awareness of what is right and good, and what is wrong and bad; what supports and enhances the human condition and what does not. And this discretion is invested more effectively if we are so educated when we are young. Carefully assaying and attuning the guidance we give our young children will help them manifest kindness and understanding as they mature. If we are concerned with the negativity society is reflecting, we must look past these signs and find the underlying, formative, source of our sickness. Legislating to admonish and discipline, while neglecting the cause of our dismay, is proving to be trivial and ineffective.

Undoubtedly history will record our time as an era of fantastic scientific achievement. In many ways we are racing out of control, developing new, more sophisticated tools, which often become outdated before we can put them to use. No need to list all the paraphernalia or mention the excitement that accompanies their acquisition. The constant intrusion of the 'material' disrupts our lives and subtly draws us away from the values and ideals we know are important, and a longed-for contemplative environment gradually slips away. No doubt one of the reasons some of us and some of our children are rebellious and unhappy is because we feel we are prisoners doomed to a material existence. Simple things, in themselves of little consequence, impose and control. Materialism is like an entrapment, a spider's web that refuses to let go. This is particularly devastating for our young people, who are endlessly being given mixed signals regarding priorities. The emphasis that society places on the importance of the material and the superficial is overwhelming. Young, receptive, and trusting minds are available to all influences, *and vulnerable*, and if we older folks, their teachers, demonstrate by our own behaviour the acceptance of questionable values and wavering principles, the consequences for the children will be predictable. We must remember they are not the producers, the manufacturers, planning and creating any of their environments. They are the ones who are receptive and waiting, eager to be taught and ready to know. And, there is no question; they are looking to us older folks for their guidelines and guidance.

But knowing this, we are the ones concocting the poison. We are making the movies, formulating the junk food, conjuring up the unrestrained, self-indulgent, superficial, ballyhooing commercials that depict, as normal and enviable, an image of approval and self-worth that can only be described as outrageous. Incredibly, with intent, we design and bring to our children, *in their homes*, films and videos that depict sensuality, brutality, and inanity without constraint. The material world is presented as the only reality and is shown in its darkest attire.

If the other non-physical existence is revealed to our young people, it is not presented in the mainstream environments where they live. Spirituality, if perceived at all, is presented as a separate consideration, one that is perhaps 'out there', but does not blend or work into the fabric of their daily lives. And certainly it is not considered to be the underlying factor that regulates all life. Somehow, we have given our children the impression that spirituality can have only a religious connotation, and this implies, apparently, a separate set of rules, a particular attitude, like being especially and appropriately restrained, considerate, even reverent.

Their everyday world of school and recreation involves lessons and activities that exercise the mind and body, but the deeper, more significant understandings regarding both of these instruments are not conveyed. In one of His discourses,[3] 'Abdu'l-Bahá clarifies the networking of spiritual energy relevant to the human condition. The following is a paraphrase of His words:

The **brain** is the instrument of the mind. The **mind** is the instrument of the soul, and it is used to fathom the mysteries, thereby enabling the soul to develop. The **human soul** is the individualized expression of the human spirit, i.e., Spirit manifested in the human kingdom degree. ('Abdu'l-Bahá designates it the *rational* soul as its capacities incorporate reason and thought.) **Spirit** itself is the wondrous, indestructible, indivisible Energy infusing life in all of existence. The terrestrially formed body is the instrument that facilitates (in this part of its journey) the soul's advancement toward enlightenment. 'Abdu'l-Bahá explains that the force we are calling Spirit is universal, is in evidence and motivates all the realms. In this context, soul is not excluded from any physical form, but is manifested particularly, with definable restriction relative to the capacity of each form. (Hence, we might designate the soul of the mineral to be the *cohesive* soul; the vegetable, the *growing, metabolizing*, soul; and the animal, the *sensitive, instinctual* soul.)

Because the material world is so much a part of daily life, our children will find it difficult to discover the evidences of Spirit without our help. It is easy, even for us older folks, to misinterpret this Energy and imagine that we ourselves are physical beings having spiritual experiences, not realizing that the reality is quite opposite – we are spiritual beings having physical experiences. If the children are unaware of the existence and availability of such abstract thoughts, like concepts must be introduced so that as they mature they will become familiar with the words and begin to have their own thoughts and then discover their own insights. In reality, our youngsters, with little or no awareness, live constantly in this spiritual world of abstraction where perception and comprehension abide; where doubt and hope are in the core of their being; and happiness and sorrow become the consequences of expectation, trust, and love. Even though these spiritual attributes work together to develop their hidden potentialities, our youngsters still may course their way through life unaware of the forces that are at work within. And why? merely because they were not informed.

To young people who have been denied access to such a perception, this may initially sound too 'far out', some sort of half-baked mumbo-jumbo that has nothing to do with their agenda. 'There are *important* things to do, like meeting friends at the Mall, surfing the Internet, or scouting around for the latest DVD. Who has time? Who needs all this spiritual stuff?'

Of course the answer is, we all do. We cannot live without it.

Family

Life, as it is presented to our consciousness, appears to be a wondrous profusion of physical shapes and sizes, spectacular colours, and incredible complexities. If someone had not mentioned the fact, we, perhaps like the rocks, flowers, and bees, might accept our existence as a purely physical one. We start our journey encapsulated in a microscopic, and (what might appear to be) rather commonplace, individual cell, and, after a mandatory confinement, are presented to (what has every sign of being) an all-encompassing physical world. Everything, our surroundings and we ourselves appear to be quite substantial. Where would we ever get the idea that there is something more going on?

Values and morals are not hidden within us when we start out. The miraculous confluence of 'simple' atoms merging at conception instils a perfect individualized human soul (i.e., the degree of spiritual Energy our material substance can tolerate) in this pristine embryonic matter. These wondrous souls are perfect but immature, vital but dormant, and will remain so, a mere potential, if they are not awakened. If, as brand new participants in the human kingdom, we are left alone, we will not survive. In the womb, our development is assured and monitored by the natural law that moves life toward maturity. Once the egg and sperm meet, this progress cannot be controlled. However, when we are born, and awaken to the realities of this physical world, our advancement is not so guaranteed.

If we are cared for, embraced and loved, nourished and sheltered, held close as a treasure placed in trust, the chances of our survival are pretty good. If our parents neglect to care for us or fail to give us guidance, this abandonment becomes an abuse and the chances of our survival are not so good. It is parents and children together – the family – that makes it work. And this simple organization is neither superficial nor optional. The cohesive structure of the family is the basic ingrained discipline organizing all the kingdoms, enabling them to function and survive.

Who knows what happens in the mineral realm – how the molecule-families behave? What manner of discipline does Spirit impose that might evoke such conditioned compliance? Do the atom's particles bond together merely because this 'love' is amenable to their 'substance'? Are their electrons and protons unable to withstand this force and cannot but comply? Words might be switched around to make the point. It might be said that the flower, to assure the longevity of the family, takes care to drop its seeds in a timely manner. Or the butterfly makes certain its eggs are attached to the right leaf so that, when the youngsters emerge, the table will be set and their essential needs will be met.

But up the scale, reasonable evidences of this structured behaviour are everywhere apparent. In the swarm, flock, or herd, Spirit organizes the caregivers to function according to a prescribed and persistent formula, and the adults diligently 'assume responsibility' for the children. In the hive, each busy bee devotes its life to the integrity of the family and has a particular function designed to assure the survival of the next generation – fanning the larvae to keep them cool, guarding the entrance to repel intruders, collecting the nectar for the hungry back home. The mother and father hawk take turns warming the eggs, then guarding the fledglings and bringing them food. In the herd, the newborn elephant cannot survive without its family. The whole community bonds together to protect the calf and is faithful to the end. This conformity is inherent in the structured substances of the lower kingdoms. The individual participants express this love without analysis or intent. Because of the oneness principle, the universality of this law implies that it must be relevant to our contemplative realm as well.

What is it that the human family stands for, and what should parents teach? The family is the simplest form of government. Within the confines of this social structure the members find much freedom, but they also understand where the parameters are and what the consequences of an infraction will be. To achieve the intent, everyone in the family sacrifices some degree of independence. The elders – parents and guardians – teach the little ones the rules that will enable this small community to achieve its objective. For the children to understand the oneness of purpose that disciplines and directs, it is incumbent upon them to acquiesce in the authority of the parents. And it is incumbent upon the parents to present to the children a *single* standard, so that the boundary lines are clearly known, and a *just* standard, designed to accommodate the individuality of each of the children.

In the home, the constraints placed on the freedom of the youngsters as they grow prepare them for their participation in the larger community waiting outside. Children should master the lessons concerning honesty, self-control and consideration for others before they enter the world where these spiritual attributes are required and expected. The social structure of the town, state, nation, and inter-nation cannot function and be productive if dishonesty, intolerance, selfishness, and greed hold sway. These moral/spiritual 'laws' are indispensable and are to be considered as a safeguard for the participants and for the community as a whole.

A oneness is established as the individuals within the group find, outside of themselves, a greater conformity that enhances the fulfilment of the universal purpose, and thus gives greater meaning to their individual lives.

Mankind is like a large family. Each participant, whether an individual, a family, a town, or a nation, finds meaning only when sacrificing subjective concerns for the more encompassing social and spiritual goal. Each member-unit becomes the concern of all the others. In the village, if a child of the village is not cared for, the village itself must become responsible. If a town or nation is under attack, whether by storm or by siege, every other town and nation must respond. If this does not happen, the neglect of the one becomes abuse by the many. The oneness of mankind is more than a comforting phrase. We human beings are meaningless without one another, without the physical and spiritual capacities that complement and enhance our own. Today, the era we are to implement is unparalleled; the Energy we are to reflect will be unprecedented. As we examine our past record and reflect on our kingdom's achievements, i.e., the fruition of tribe, clan, and nation, with their commensurate degrees of maturity, we can anticipate our next step. With a bit more evolution, when human capacities are again quickened and the oneness of mankind is firmly established, when *all the kingdoms* then function with complementary and reciprocal harmony, our small planet will become a gem in the diadem of the universe.

Oneness

The achievement of ultimate purpose – do we dare to believe this can happen? To an impartial observer, not necessarily one from outer space, it would appear that we (you and I) have dropped in on our kingdom's development at a most auspicious time. Our ancestors, way back, abiding by the requisites of the evolutionary process, wrenching their way out of rudimentary physical and intellectual bondage, then struggling with the disciplines imposed in the ascent of clan to nation, did surprisingly well, and we thank them. They carried the torch of progress to our time, and though they may not have been aware of their mission, the oneness of mankind was, it now would seem, predestined and inevitable – providing we do not destroy ourselves in these final moments.

At the time of this writing, humanity is suffering agonies beyond comprehension. Our capacities for love and beneficence are overcome by fear and suspicion, and the consequences are unbearable. And unacceptable, for our lives are much too precious; they have much greater worth. Prejudice, initially unknown to little children, is taught worldwide from the outset, and thereafter taints their perception of the world. Hate and anger, terror and privations of every kind are presented to our children as a routine state of affairs. In the dark of so long a night the children can have no assurance that there is to be a dawn. The view that they are caught up in a transition, that they are witnessing the death of an old era and the birth of a new, is withheld from them. Their restrained vision does not allow the insight that what they are seeing and hearing are the cries and torment of tribal and national societies being unwillingly transformed into a global community. The death throes and birth pangs intertwine as mankind holds fast to outdated systems. The introduction and intrusion of diversity, ethnic and religious, is perceived as a cause of dissension, and the children of the day find it almost impossible to become aligned with the oneness inherent in the new era. Because of the tediousness of this emergence, the burden of disassociation may hold mankind‘s spiritual destiny prisoner a while longer, but the children, if carefully taught, will understand and prevail.

And, as well, our infatuation with technology, along with the accompanying and generally perceived notion that 'things' have intrinsic value, is committing us all to a lop-sided existence. To be instrumental in bringing stability and meaning to our children's lives during this transition time, our first job as parents and teachers is to lure them away from the clutches of materialism. But if we are to wean them off computer games and sugared cereals, we must do more than buy them books and serve them oatmeal. The new education must extend beyond the normal learning processes and academic disciplines, for ultimately it is to align the children's capacities with the synthesis of life, and thereby change the world. The tricks of numbers and the magic of words, as important as they are, will be acknowledged simply as tools to fathom the mysteries.

Although the curriculum will address the imparting of common and current knowledge, it will approach that knowledge from a different point of view. It will make available to the children the opportunity to become acquainted with the *essential nature* of the familiar systems, particularly those enabling and disciplining their own lives. If this inquiry is withheld from their education, they will naturally assume that such investigations and findings, whatever they might be, are unimportant and irrelevant to their developmental needs.

Such insight can be presented with neutrality, without bias, through meaningful lessons, exciting experiments, and constructive activities. The puzzling indefinable Energy locked within the atom is worthy of note, a wonderful point of reference, for it is here that the mysteries begin; the secrets hidden in the minerals, plants, and animals will be awe-inspiring; but in the whole spectrum of life, the non-physical identity of physical matter is, of course, *most apparent and most abundantly bestowed* in the make-up of our young people themselves.

We, their parents and teachers, cannot assign to others (for there are no others) the responsibility of sharing such vision. It falls upon us to find a curriculum and an agenda that will help our young people discover their station, their sphere of function, and then their obligation. There can be no doubt that the intellectual energy channelling through the oncoming generations will stimulate questions, and we must be ready to help them find answers. In the algebra class, when Nkoroge is staring off into space, and is called back, where has he been? What terms might we use to describe that place of visitation? And what part of Nkoroge went there? Did his cerebral atoms play a part in taking him away from the classroom and the immediacy of his lessons, or was it something else? Good questions? No doubt, but apparently not questions for the classroom.

When the bell rings, and the students move down the hall to the science class, they will study about the basic structure of physical matter, about the electric energy locked within the atoms forming the structure of everything in the universe. As they gradually become acquainted with this fascinating subject, they will be carried away on a magic carpet of speculations. For example: The alignment of the particles – the atoms – that make up their shoes and the floor their shoes are standing on is almost identical. And, as astounding as it might seem, these particles are widely distanced from each other, not unlike the structure of the heavens above with the myriad stars scattered remotely throughout an eternity. Their question: 'Why don't our shoes filter through the floor?'

A curricular consideration of the spiritual nature of physical matter can bring meaning to lives that have hitherto been imagined to be meaningless. Enthusiasm will overcome indifference, and the desire to venture into the world of abstraction will enkindle our children's souls and then illumine their world. Undoubtedly it will encourage the youthful seekers to examine anew the wonders of nature. Our youngsters cannot observe their own inner selves, but like-patterns are mirrored in the worlds surrounding them, and these *are* available for study. That pollywog in the forest pond can become a spiritual adventure, leading not only to a realization that the equilibrium and survival of the pond depends upon the bonding of each pollywog to its surroundings, but that the over-abundance or scarcity of any of the pond's constituents, pollywogs included, will drastically upset the natural balance. Discussions of the environment, or of the consequences of one's actions, can ensue.

When Spirit (remember, this is my word) is recognized as the incomprehensible force motivating all forms, an attitude of respect and even awe will be forthcoming. Abuse of the surrounding environments will be unthinkable. Rather, a behaviour reflecting courtesy and honour will be directed to all systems. Because the pollywog, the pond, and the forest itself manifest life's effulgence in comparatively restricted degrees, they will invite reverence, for they reflect *perfectly* and *completely* the degree of Energy relevant to their kingdom and their kind. When the children acknowledge that life, as an essence, is universal and indivisible, and is expressed through matter with wonderful and limitless particularity, they will discover oneness. And they will find a personal relationship with every living form, even with the soil of the earth, with those amazing particles that comprise their own substance, enable their thoughts, and allow their dreams.

Because Spirit is reflected with originality by the extraordinarily formulated materials that are conjoined when each plant, animal, and human being is 'conceived', the young students will be able to understand why there is so much diversity manifested in life. In their inquiry into the essential nature of each species, new perceptions will be born. What we define as 'sex' will be revealed as a miraculous process demonstrating the existence of a spiritual reality clearly beyond comprehension. Vegetable, animal, or human: whatever the kingdom, *when the male and female particles meet and merge, because of the identity of the atoms involved and the method and manner of their configuration, the ensuing pristine substance brings into existence evidences of Spirit in ways and degrees that are unprecedented.* When the children conclude that the atoms are merely pawns used to evoke particular non-physical effects, new insights will enrich their lives.

Although not in evidence in the formative years, the charge and claim of responsibility is inborn in each child's constitution. At conception Spirit takes residence in the most complex material that can be assembled. Held within is the ultimate commission, for it is here that physical matter is called upon to enable free will and capacitate responsibility. When delivered from the womb, each precious child is, in a sense, charged with the obligation of manifesting spiritual qualities through the employment of the dust of the universe. When the new baby arrives, we all marvel and wonder at its perfection. But then, early in its journey, when the little one is just starting out, we encourage it to compare its own bestowals with those possessed by others. Why do we do this? We all know this tiny tot has more important things to do with its unique capacities and its allotted time.

The newborn child may be truly miraculous, but this is just the beginning, there is much more marvel to come. As the days pass, every great and small event that presents itself to this bundle of Energy produces a consequence that can neither be predicted nor disavowed, for what is to transpire has never happened before – and this, then, becomes the cause of another effect, and so on and on. The happenstance of composition and then the vicissitudes of each child's particular journey disclose a life that will not be open to criticism. Putting the youngster through a scholastic processing mill, molding natural endowments to measure up to predetermined and impersonal standards of 'normality' must be considered, again, an abuse. Spirit needs unrestricted access to assure individuality. Can we imagine the anguish of a soul, destined for particularity, its enabling particles so specific and so arranged as to evoke spiritual attributes freely and naturally, shackled all the while by conformity?

Becoming aware of the non-physical realities working through the physical presentation will introduce all of us to the deeper meanings. We should be our brothers' keepers, but why? And why is it not just a nice idea that we love one another? It is because humanity is, and is to be regarded as, a single organism, a cellular community that can function and be productive only when undivided. Like variegated threads woven into cloth, into the fabric of life itself, all are needed for its strength and beauty. Our differences of capacity and kind are equal to our number, and no one takes precedence over another. We vary. During any particular phase of our realm's evolution, the spiritual emanation manifested is commensurate to the degree of Energy channelled by each participant. It matters little that individual capacities differ; one equivalent, perhaps, to a gallon measure, another to a cup, for the capacities themselves do not have correspondence; they are the same only in that they progress from an undisclosed particularized potential toward fulfilment. Though distinct, each wayfarer's journey is commissioned similarly: with our free will, we are to choose whatever is conducive to the enhancement of the human condition. Other concerns are to be put aside. The lifting of the human spirit, our Spirit, becomes everyone's particular responsibility.

If our children can grasp the concept of the oneness of mankind and the unity of existence, they will readily understand why they themselves are responsible, not only for the blossoming of their own lives, or even of the lives of others, but of life itself. Why should the children not allow themselves to be cheated? It is because they become partners in allowing the offender to harm himself. If they are shortchanged by a total stranger and do not call attention to the infraction, they – by their participation – become involved, responsible, and culpable. If even only one individual's spiritual condition is in jeopardy the integrity of the entire kingdom becomes weakened, compromised. And as well, if any of the natural environments are in jeopardy, for any reason, but particularly because of human abuse or error, our children must understand the responsibility they have for restoring the natural balance. Again, they must be informed.

To understand how we, with our diversities, can adapt to the singleness of purpose implied in the human condition (i.e., the achievement of human goals) requires insight into the nature of our inborn capacities. How we, as multifaceted and dissimilar individuals, relate to and take part in the manifestation of the one consistent human presentation is an important consideration, especially for our children, for they are aware mostly of their own disparities. For us, as teachers, this should not be a difficult assignment. The youngster's so-called differences are insignificant when measured against their homogeneity. Their essential humanity, outwardly clothed in colourful but superficial attire, is endowed with basic and universal kingdom qualities. Despite their individuality, they are quite similar physically *and* spiritually. Their body tissues and fluids are generally proportional, and often compatible, and nourishment and warmth are needed by all. And certainly the necessity of an environment that acknowledges and supports their intellectual/spiritual well-being is shared universally.

Those differences that are meaningful become apparent within the context of oneness, wherein individual diversity presents a spectrum of capacity that can be found only in the human kingdom. Diversity in the other realms is manifested in the endless variety of species that make up the mineral, vegetable, and animal worlds, but there is very little distinction within each species. A chunk of obsidian is a definite mineral composition; it has all the properties identifying it as an inorganic substance, but it is certainly not the only inorganic substance. The philodendron is a wonderful plant, but, of course, it is not the only plant. An animal may be a small chipmunk, but there are lots of other animals.

This is not so with us. The human kingdom embraces just one species, actually just one family, with all these unique individuals. Some of us may be Polynesians, but there are no duplicates. In the vast sea of humankind, each one of us is an island individual.

****

The neutrality of this offering is appealing, and fair, for it does not impair the children's freedom to view their world and themselves objectively. Once they acknowledge the existence of Energy/Spirit and the part it plays in directing physical matter toward enhancement, they will, with their minds in motion, discover the importance of directing their own lives forward and upward. They will pick and choose those verities that will enhance their own condition and therewith enrich the world. This kind of education *can* take place in the classroom.

This programme leaves the way open for parents who want, or do not want, their children to be guided by doctrine or faith. This judgement and responsibility is removed from the classroom and referred to the home. The proposal honours the separation of church and state (an important issue in my part of the world), for the study of nature's laws is without a secular or other particularized agenda. This impartiality does not imply a resigning of obligations; rather, it allows the children the freedom to direct their own lives as they gradually become aware of the incumbency of the quest.

Reality

Human awareness is distinguished by the degree of insight manifested at a particular time. In our cave-man days, we might have been mindful of the relationship of a primal cause to a consequent effect; the one designing and compelling; the other responding and reflecting. Perhaps, even back then, we were able to acknowledge our station of dependence rather than one of omniscience – that we were part of the effect, the consequence of something greater than we were. But, since knowledge of the 'realm of cause' is closed to the capacities of the 'realm of effect', it follows that we human beings, no matter what our era, cannot comprehend, in any regard, the essential nature of the organized phenomena called life. However, in this scientific age, we *are* able to recognize that energy (Energy) is the underlying factor enabling the display of existence. This knowledge leads us away from a reliance on rational scientific proofs to a different mental/spiritual environment wherein we can direct our search for truth with greater success.

That we can, through comprehension, begin to glean anything of spiritual matters is remarkable in itself. We can say this because, until recently, historically most of our knowledge has been limited to the material world. Evolution has developed our physical and mental capabilities in wondrous ways, but our own non-physical reality, as well as the non-physical identity of life in general, has remained mysterious. Our rituals of the past disclose that we had little knowledge of the forces at work within the physical presentation; technology was to come later. But looking back, we are somewhat dismayed that the early peoples, with so much less information, realized their own spiritual orientation better that we do ours today. With less distraction, perhaps not so burdened by 'things', their connection to the oneness was more clearly defined, enabling them to respond naturally with an ordered and adaptable way of life.

In their search for *their own* spiritual orientation, our children cannot revert to an earlier time, for it is their generation that is caught up in the global maturation. The accelerating tempo of quickening intellectual awareness, coupled with the gathering and merging of the world's diverse and separate cultures, is calling for a response never before required. Our youngsters' task is one of reassessment. If they think that matters of the spirit are merely dreamy fantasies, the new education will help them find more satisfying interpretations. The non-physical aspects of life may be incomprehensible, but they are not unreal.

The consequences of such a reappraisal will bring to the classroom the excitement of discovery. The children will be set ablaze as they introduce themselves to basic fundamentals, the discovery of what is *real* and what is not. As inscrutable as it may seem, insight can come into being *instantly*, unannounced, with stunning and glistening clarity, and when it does come, the new vision will reveal the physical world to be an illusion, its worth, in itself, comparable to 'the black in the eye of a dead ant'.[4] All the evidences, what they hear, and see, and feel will become windows to their understanding and will allow the radiance of hidden meaning to light their way. Oh yes, the physical world looks so real. It feels so real and it sounds so real. But today, the tools of discovery we have fashioned have rendered obsolete the reliability of our perceptions based on our senses. We know that light, sound, and substance are inherent qualities of creation, and, yes, our senses enable us to analyse these mysteries, but only to a limited degree. In many ways our sensory capabilities filter and restrict our comprehension of the real identity of the worlds that surround us.

A speculation

Out of the stuff of the universe our earth was conceived and born. The material composition was not lifeless; life is inherent in physical matter, and what was to evolve in the future was determined by what was present in the past. As with the seed and the flower, our earth could not produce forces and structures differently derived from, and not relevant to, its original pristine potential. We in our human kingdom waited an eternity for the development of the environments that would sustain us, and, since the time of our emergence, our realm has been adapting to the imposed physical and spiritual evolution.

So, now, here we are all excited about travelling to the far reaches of the universe. We take with us everything we have become, but our earth-evolved tools may not disclose the evidences we hope to find in what could be a differently derived environment. We function well with our technology and our perception here at home, but our capacities are terrestrial. We have no idea of the nature or number of the energies that surround us, even pass through us. Our inborn receptors gather the waves and pulses so that our intellect can organize them into meanings, and our invented receptors pick up the radio, television, and x-ray vibrations, but who can know what undiscovered and never-to-be uncovered mysteries are around, through, and within? We cannot comprehend any of the realities. We recognize the signs and then attribute meanings. The dimensions of life are most likely endless, and we, with our finite capabilities, can at most merely touch on their particularities and attributes.

Our earth-sight, for example, responds to a very narrow spectrum of the sun's total energy. This measurable band, which registers on the energy chart between the infrared and ultraviolet wavelengths, is called 'visible light'.

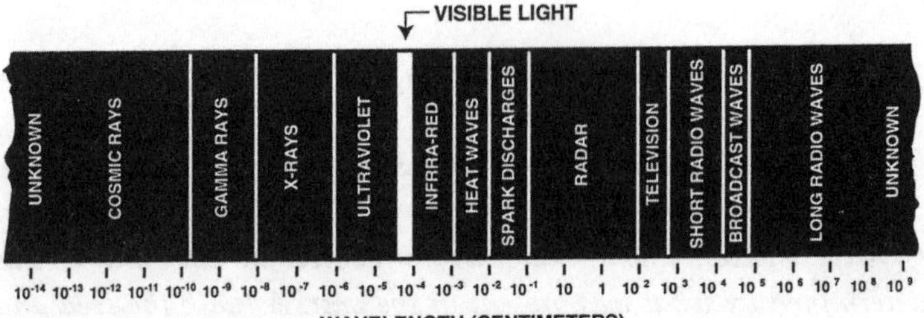

Wavelength Chart

It is obvious that our eyes, fashioned with 'the materials at hand', suppress most of the 'lights' of the world and consequently what we perceive of the reality of existence is distorted and enfeebled by our organ of sight. Taking our terrestrial vision to a far distant world, we might miss that planetary presentation and come back to report, 'Too bad. No one was there.' Back here in our own world, our perception of the realities around us would be very odd indeed if our eyes were structured just a little differently and we were to make our way with infrared, ultraviolet, or gamma sight.

There are so many mysteries. That the magnitude of life should be manifested through several and specific categories or kingdoms is certainly an elemental one. Perhaps, in the achievement of purpose, the flow of Energy from mineral to man necessitates the intermediate capacities to facilitate, as economically as possible, the required transitions. Be that as it may, the mineral, vegetable, animal, and human realms embrace all forms, and their interdependence is flawless and absolute. The substances employed are perfectly formulated to invite remarkable effects, and they are easily identified, as we have seen in the example on page 17. In case you missed it, here it is again. If the children were given some material to hold in their cupped hands, and it had shape only, it quickly would be identified as a mineral substance, a piece of granite or a ball of mercury. (Of course, children could not do this today, but when I was a youngster, no one realized how dangerous mercury really is.) If the subject matter were growing, perhaps photosynthesizing, they would have no trouble naming it a plant of some kind. If the material could sense or feel, if it turned to lick, or lunged to bite, the youngsters would say, 'This assortment is definitely an animal.' Although too large to hold in cupped hands, if the assembled conglomeration were busy thinking about things and (most likely) worrying about things, this very complicated composite would be called a human being – no kinds, no classification – just a human being. Actually, all the samples are pretty much the same: countless atoms assembled in endless combinations so that Spirit can express itself in a world of substance.

Immortality

Interestingly, so long as a natural and befitting configuration and balance is maintained within each structure, Spirit will reside there and manifest that particular degree of life. If circumstances from without or within intervene, or the normal longevity is attained, the chemistry of the substance begins to change, and the plant, animal, and you and I start to devitalize and then die. The inhibiting of Spirit *in a particular degree* comes to all living forms when the physical substance is no longer an appropriate environment for its residence. Oftentimes, during the life cycle of all these forms, because of privation or illness, Spirit will be less apparent, its evidence repressed, until the substance's integrity is reestablished – given water or nourishment, perhaps a dietary supplement, even a gentle touch or encouraging word. When this happens, Spirit can again become fully displayed. We call this 'a recovery'. Actually, it is a recovery of the *capacity of the enabling substance* to disclose the spiritual presence. Spirit could never take leave of the substance, for the atoms within are always vibrantly alive with its energy, ready to accommodate any purpose, anywhere, any time.

The relationship of Spirit and physical matter can be a fascinating disclosure – the degree of life expressed being dependent upon the representation and organization of the basic constituent particles. If in our laboratories we were able to gather specific atoms and arrange them so perfectly that they would accommodate and manifest life, not only as they might in the mineral degree, but as they might in the vegetable, animal, and human degree, we would be able to 'create' life. Well, almost. Actually, we wouldn't be creating life; there isn't a place in creation where life steps outside of physical matter. It is not possible, where physical substance abides, that life is not already there. To really create life, we would have to search around and find a substance to work with where life is not inherently instilled – but this is not possible. What we would actually be doing is manipulating some live mineral atoms so that they would then relate to each other in such ways that Spirit would be able to enhance its residence. We would then have a rock, or a plant, or an animal – or a human being, depending on the degree of perfection resulting as a consequence of our tinkering.

In the laboratory, looking through the microscope, we can actually watch the process called life. We can see the cells dividing, multiplying, and vibrating with Energy – we can witness miracles extending far beyond our wildest dreams. In their science class, our young students will be fascinated with the inner workings of their everyday commonplace world. Gathering around a simple demonstration, they will actually witness the presence and power of Spirit hiding within the physical presence. Sylvie, one of the bright-eyed researchers, will be asked to help with the experiment. The teacher will give her a small live sponge and a fine-mesh screen and, with a little help, she will gently push the body of the sponge through the screen with such care that the individual members of that cellular community will be separated from each other, but not injured. Then, Sylvie and her classmates will watch spellbound as the resultant mushy mess reassembles itself into its original social structure and continues with its life, much as it was planning to do before it was so rudely interrupted.

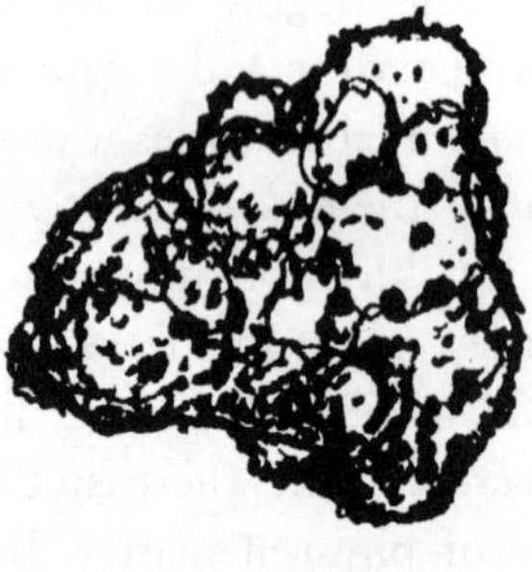

Crossing over to another table, our budding biologists will direct their attention to a small aquarium, and, looking carefully, they will find the tiny hydra waving its 'arms'around, searching for something to eat. But there isn't any food, for the water is clean and clear, and this little aquatic creature is no doubt wondering where its next meal is coming from. Mindful of its delicate constitution, the teacher will transfer it to a different tank and place it on some agar jelly at the bottom (yummy). This is much better; going out to eat is always fun. However, hungry or not, bad table manners have a consequence. Our little hydra leans over and its mouth opens so wide that its rubbery, tubular body flips inside out. What a dilemma! But what happens next is quite unbelievable. The cells

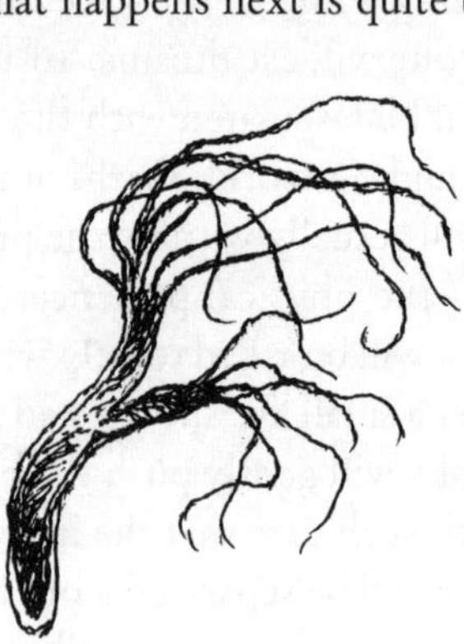

that compose its exterior, and those that form its internal parts, switch places, transposing themselves, passing through one another (as I remember, much like Chicago's busy noontime crowd going to lunch), and this amazing little creature will retrieve its original sylphlike figure. Having watched it go through such an ordeal, our youngsters undoubtedly will turn their attention to themselves and thereafter watch their own table manners more closely.

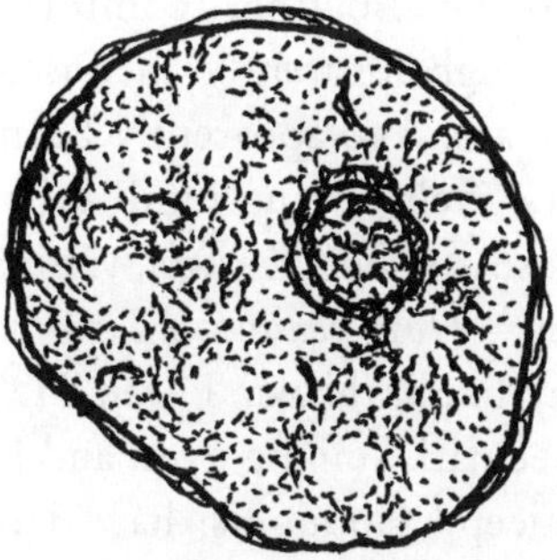

Another experiment is waiting for our students. Taking turns at the microscope, they will focus on the one-celled amoeba aimlessly 'swimming' in its tiny ocean. As it bumps into 'this', somehow sensing 'that', the students will see life at work (in the animal degree). If, as they watch, its watery world dries up and this microscopic miracle loses its home, they can witness the process called death; the pulsing movements suddenly stop. But wait, did life really cease to exist? If the lens is powerful enough, our young researchers will see that life's Energy is still very much there, locked in the whirling atoms all charged up and ready to go.

Changing the magnification again, making the image smaller, the children will see the dried-up body of their recently departed friend, and they will wonder and ponder. 'Could we possibly reverse the process – restore its environment and then have those mineral atoms reflect life in the animal degree once again? Would a drop of water bring our tiny amoeba back from wherever it has been? Sounds kind of tricky. We would have to make sure the atoms are aligned properly, just as they were before the drought. Maybe the slightest electrical jolt would set the machinery in motion and the mineral atoms will be our bumping-around-buddy once more.'

Just for fun, let's imagine I am the subject being scrutinized. I'm on the table in the examining room, and a bustling crew is busy with their tubes and needles (hmm, not as much fun as I thought it would be). Their activities are in sharp contrast to my own. I seem to be floating, comfortably detached and unconcerned. Although apparently unconscious, I sense 'feeling' and, somehow, can see. And apparently I can hear, for the words 'We're losing him – we're losing him!' drift my way. It doesn't really matter because . . . '*Oh! The light, yes, there's the light, and the peace, oh, the peace – How beautiful! I am home, I am safe*,' and then, from far away, like a whisper, I hear, 'He's coming back. He's back.' I wake to see dark smiling eyes, and I hear, 'Hello. You're fine now, go to sleep.' Goodness, have I been away? Did the adrenaline and electric shock rearrange my atoms so that I might use them again? Where do I go when I sleep? Where do I go when I die?

Spirit does not 'go somewhere' when death occurs. It is always in attendance. It does not move about, traversing a distance from here to there. Its total energy is ever intact. Wherever existence exists, Spirit becomes known. 'Abdu'l-Bahá explains:

> Some think that the body is the substance and exists by itself, and that the spirit is accidental and depends upon the substance of the body, although, on the contrary, the rational soul is the substance, and the body depends upon it. If the accident – that is to say, the body – be destroyed, the substance, the spirit remains.
>
> Second, the rational soul, meaning the human spirit, does not descend into the body – that is to say, it does not enter it, for descent and entrance are characteristics of bodies, and the rational soul is exempt from this. The spirit never entered this body, so in quitting it, it will not be in need of an abiding-place: no, the spirit

> is connected with the body, as the light is with this mirror. When the mirror is clear and perfect, the light of the lamp will be apparent in it, and when the mirror becomes covered with dust or breaks, the light will disappear.[5]

And might we venture to add, the relationship is not unlike the sound of the falling tree; concentric waves come into existence as it crashes, but are secret unless the capacity of hearing is present to record the energy as sound. It is clear that Spirit exists without the physical substance, and needs it only to reveal its presence.

Thus, when the plant dies, Spirit releases the elements from the vegetable kingdom to serve again in the mineral realm and wait for their next assignment. The vegetable's 'mirror' ceases to exist. But the non-physical capacities that were reflected never die; they are perpetual and prevail in the realm of eternal mysteries.

When the chipmunk dies, Spirit in the animal degree can no longer direct the chipmunk-substance-atoms to sniff about and pick up acorns. There has been a transformation, and, although it may look like that enchanting little creature, nonetheless, it is now merely an assortment of mineral atoms dressed up in very fancy attire. Its non-physical capacities continue to reside, as they always have, in the spiritual realm; its material particles 'go home'. No doubt they will be needed again to fulfil a pollywog or a tree, or human purpose as life unfolds its plan.

The same reassignment takes place when we human beings die. When our bodies reach the end of their life cycles, or are rendered inappropriate for Spirit's (human degree of) residence, they are put aside and recycled. The mineral realm reclaims the atoms that were used to accommodate intellect and free will. But what happens to *us*, to our *spiritual attributes,* our *intellective identities,* our *reasoning realities*, and our *perceptive personalities*? To find the answer, we have tried everything we can think of – séances with marvellous mediums, spiritualists seeing into the great beyond through a crystal ball, even with whimsical ouija boards – but the beyond is beyond comprehension. However, because existence is all-embracing, both of its defining, intertwining, material and spiritual aspects must be loyal to truth. Remembering our school lessons of years ago, we recall that energy, inherent in physical matter, cannot be created or destroyed; it can only be transformed from one condition to another. It requires merely the reassignment of this energy to a non-physical, spiritual, identity to understand that *all* the kingdoms' defining capacities are indestructible. This insight is an important consideration for our children to contemplate, for it will introduce them to the whole concept of the essential non-physical identity of physical matter. This redefining leads us to conclude that Energy/Spirit, categorically named (when assigned to physical matter) cohesion, growth, sense perception, and intellect, exists without the physical presentation. It is ever in readiness, and when physical matter is called upon to serve a particular, inscrutable, need, these capacities are put to work. Spirit is immutable, preexistent. On our planet, whatever form or capacity is needed to sustain the plan must take up residence as a mineral, vegetable, animal, or human being. In this regard, if we recognize that Spirit, in all its degrees of manifestation, is perpetual and eternal, and that since our kingdom's identifying quality – intellect – can be manifested *only* through individual allocations with commensurate displays of particularized achievement, we must assume that we too, as individuals, are everlasting.

'Abdu'l-Bahá states:

> The logical proof of the immortality of the spirit is this, that no sign can come from a nonexisting thing – that is to say, it is impossible that from absolute nonexistence signs should appear – for the signs are the consequence of an existence, and the consequence depends upon the existence of the principle. So from a nonexisting sun no light can radiate; from a nonexisting sea no waves appear; from a nonexisting cloud no rain falls; a nonexisting tree yields no fruit; a nonexisting man neither manifests nor produces anything. Therefore, as long as signs of existence appear, they are a proof that the possessor of the sign is existent.[6]

And again:

> Know that nothing which exists remains in a state of repose – that is to say, all things are in motion. Everything is either growing or declining; all things are either coming from nonexistence into being, or going from existence into nonexistence. So this flower, this hyacinth, during a certain period of time was coming from the world of nonexistence into being, and now it is going from being into nonexistence. This state of motion is said to be essential – that is, natural; it cannot be separated from beings because it is their essential requirement, as it is the essential requirement of fire to burn.
>
> Thus it is established that this movement is necessary to existence, which is either growing or declining. Now, as spirit continues to exist after death, it necessarily progresses or declines; and in the other world to cease to progress is the same as to decline; but it never leaves its own condition, in which it continues to develop . . .[7]

Well, 'Abdu'l-Bahá's words set our minds in motion. Let's see if I can come close: The human condition (i.e. our essential spiritual reality) is natural and fixed, as is the spiritual condition of the mineral, plant, and animal. However, the *individuality* of the human soul establishes its immortality. Regardless of the particular circumstances of our lives, even if we are merely newly conceived, we live 'forever'. When our bodies die, are released and returned, our reality continues to abide in its natural non-physical realm. However, although designed to progress in this spiritual environment, if for some reason the soul's growth stops, its condition will in a sense regress, for it is incumbent that movement takes place. It is also stipulated that the soul's sphere of function will always be defined by the degree of Energy allowed and allotted to our kingdom. We cannot step outside of the limitations it imposes on us, share with and become a part of the creative source. As part of the *effect*, we will never attain the *cause*. (In Chapters 64, 66, and 67 of *Some Answered Questions*, Abdu'l-Bahá discusses the progress of the individual human soul after death.)

Now, let us continue with the children's everlastingness: When a child is conceived, this event is not just another inconsequential tick of the evolutionary clock. Spirit may direct the progress of life, using the atoms over and over, engineering the kingdoms to select their substances and evolve according to the rules of the inscrutable plan, but when a human being is formulated from this universal dust, the whole spectrum of life is instilled with purpose. At the enigmatic moment of conception, the human spirit (i.e., Spirit reflected by physical matter to the human degree) is instantly infused in what is to be a wondrous material/spiritual presence. This astounding configuration of atoms is the beginning of a life that holds within its substance the purpose of life itself. In this elemental assemblage there has been placed a supreme trust, for it is only through its existence that the existence of the whole can be discovered, acknowledged, and be made meaningful.

The womb, our first home, is the perfect environment. Nothing is lacking. The nourishment and protection of the tiny human being are, herein, naturally and unequivocally provided, and the universal law immediately orchestrates this womb-child's development. In an amazingly short period of time (you can tell a mother didn't write this), this infant develops all the primary tools it will need to function in the world waiting outside. Actually, its birth into this earthly environment could be considered its second entry, the first being the awakening, in the womb, of its human reality from the vital material/spiritual resources of the universe.

However, in the moment of our conception Spirit is not only disclosed in a human form, but it is given for its playground a combination of elements that has never existed before. The promise of this material's propensity to spiritual enlightenment is unknown. The gene pools of the parents, residing in the uniquely formulated chemistry of egg and sperm, provide Spirit a golden opportunity. Held in trust within this earthen matter, human capacities lie in wait. The significance of an individual conception is far from insignificant, for each convergence provides the means to reveal unprecedented and often particularly relevant capacity for achievement. The *effect* wondrously facilitates the cause as Spirit moves the entirety forward.

Spirit, instilled in the womb-child, is perfect and will abide forever. However, when born into the physical world this precious soul could become in jeopardy, for its parents and teachers will now have the responsibility of guiding the new arrival through its formative, determining years. This 'education' they undertake is directed ultimately toward the achievement of enlightenment. This is to be considered the goal for those who are to care for us initially, and of course for those of us who are able to care for ourselves later on.

As we mature we can, because of our free will, choose to cultivate our own capacities and direct their development toward fulfilment, though certainly we can elect to do just the opposite and therewith disrupt the whole process. It is clear that our souls should be molded to reflect the contributory, positive, qualities lying potentially in the capacities of our kingdom, for we can most assuredly develop negatively.

Like our first womb-world that prepared us for the terrestrial journey, this earthly setting is to be perceived (many of us believe) as the perfect environment for our introduction to the spiritual nature of (what we define as) reality. Here on this plane, as souls equipped with our kingdom tools of discovery, we are charged with the responsibility of filtering through the extraneous matter to find the spiritual treasure. As we are to care for our own condition, we must assume responsibility as quickly as possible. Taking care of our bodies and minds is mandatory, so that they can serve us with as few handicaps as possible as we search for our spiritual goals. Our spiritual condition when we are conceived and born is flawless, and it should be obvious that through either carelessness or intention we can interfere in its development, restrict Spirit's reflection by 'clouding our mirrors' with addictive substances or crippling thoughts that alter Energy's natural flow.

Dare we imagine the consequences when human mirrors are so glossed over that our allotment of Energy not only diminishes but disappears?

Those of us who believe that this force is non-existent, that the physical world comprises the whole package, have no problem. We can 'eat, drink, and be merry, for tomorrow we die'. We can 'let the chips fall where they may – we only live once'. There is no struggle here. But those of us who have concluded, through various

Challenge? What challenge?

convictions, that this terrestrial journey is but an episode, perhaps a prelude to a continuing existence, battle endlessly with the moral issues that ensue. Weighing every thought, considering every action in the light of its influence, beneficial or detrimental, on our spiritual condition and the condition of our fellow human beings, our kingdom, is, we feel, a full-time job.

However, the prospect of a spiritual advantage to replace a worldly restraint is not the only incentive disciplining our behaviour. We who believe in a spiritual reality willingly choose a regulated life because there is then the likelihood that such a path will lead us into closer proximity with the oneness of purpose that is so unerringly expressed by the other kingdoms. We perceive that bringing ourselves into such conformity will bring order, peace, and purpose to our lives.

Disciplining our lives to comply with the structured behaviour of the other realms does, however, necessitate the 'giving up' of one thing for another. The lessons gleaned from observing the natural patterns universally displayed leads us to an understanding of the meaning of sacrifice. Since we are an inseparable part of the whole, the rule of sacrifice must apply to us as well.

Sacrifice

This speculation about the role of sacrifice becomes an inquiry into the nature of one of the universal laws. In order for life to express itself and develop toward a goal, one condition must be relinquished for another. The law dictates that nothing can remain stationary or the same. And the sacrifice always leads toward the achievement of purpose. The seed gives way to the tree; the dawn is sacrificed for the day; youth is lost but maturity is gained. Unawareness to enlightenment, simplicity to complexity, unfinished to completed, clan to nation, inspiration to invention, sickness to recovery – natural harmony, monitored by Spirit, directs both material and spiritual development forward, and this progression calls for one state of being to be surrendered in favour of another.

A good example of this evolving transforming process, the advancement of life through renunciation, is demonstrated by observing the rebirth of physical matter and the ascent of spiritual condition that is constantly taking place in the different kingdoms. (It is normally called the food chain.) In order for the minerals, the substance of the earth, to become a part of the next higher degree of existence, they must 'sacrifice' their soil-bound capacities and be reborn in the verdant vitality of the vegetable realm. It is here that the miraculous ascent takes place. The plant 'reaches down' and 'lifts' the mineral particles into a more enhanced environment and these particles then participate in the spiritual processes we call metabolism. The wonder of this phenomenon cannot be overstated, for the atoms themselves are not aware of the part they are playing, nor can they effect the metamorphosis alone – lift themselves up by their own boot straps. And the plant cannot direct the process intentionally, for its capacities do not embrace a will. It is a part of the grand educational plan that bestows purpose overall.

Moving up the scale, the law is universally relevant. To amplify its attribute of growth, the plant kingdom (its atoms assembled as the ultimate vegetarian buffet) is reborn in the animal condition and its basic particles then express sense perception and instinctual behaviour. But when the particles are in this animated state (with its no-place-to-go repetition), they are essentially without purpose until born again as intellect and free will. This graduated discipline, which brings existence from its simplest to its most advanced state, is in reality a process of amplification.

All the kingdoms' spiritual properties – cohesion, growth, sense perception and intellect – are to be considered constraining capacities, limiting the display of the spiritual presence, for Spirit itself, its essence and wholeness, is beyond exhibition and expression. Its reality is unknown and unknowable. However, the *evidence* of Spirit's existence and supremacy is exemplified in the perfection of the attributes of the different kingdoms: cohesion is second to none, growth is faultless, instinct is unrivalled, and intellect is exemplary. But unless there is an abiding purpose, an ultimate meaning, these attributes and their appearance are of little consequence.

To consummate the full cycle wherein Spirit processes physical matter to its *ultimate purpose*, we, the ones who can facilitate comprehension, must also be lifted up into a more enhanced spiritual condition. Intellect must be awakened with awareness, thinking must prepare the way for understanding. When this happens, when the mind, the tool of the soul, is alerted and aligned, Spirit is manifested through the capacities of *all the kingdoms* and ultimate purpose is achieved. And of course, the lower kingdoms rejoice when we their guardians comply, for it is then that their constraining capacities, and in fact their very existence, become meaningful. It is then that the diversity in creation is able to present its one reality.

So far so good, but what constitutes 'enlightenment' for mankind? Mastering the tools of intellect and then directing its energy toward self-serving and divisive goals certainly is not evoking correspondence in any regard. The surrounding systems are not rejoicing and being fulfilled as we pollute *their* waters, destroy *their* forests, and poison *their* air. And, needless to say, our kingdom's capabilities and objectives are severely impaired by our own self-inflicted and relentlessly abusive behaviour. Let us put reason to work. When the lower kingdoms are lifted up, their spiritual condition is advanced. What is it that we must do that will not only awaken our capacities and set our minds in motion but will fill our lives with meaning? What manner of sacrifice must we make that will enhance our station?

The answer is easy. Aimless wandering and trivial pursuits will mark our way unless we draw freely from the wellspring that sustains all life. The water is universal, but mankind is called upon to acknowledge its purity and drink from its source.

Creator?

Because we human beings can consider all the evidence displayed and recognize the order that defines creation, we are ever emboldened to look further for the cause of it all. But certainties are hard to come by. The astrophysicist scrutinizes and appraises his scholarly deductions, looking to the galaxies for signs and proofs. The physiologist dissects subatomic particles with religious fervour. And religion itself, though affirming the existence of a Creator, offers little convincing evidence of the being of such a being. And then, of course, no one has 'come back' to enlighten us regarding the nature or even the existence of 'the eternal', or of the meaning or identity of (what some of us call) the divine presence. No doubt, our speculations may be only the workings of minds illumined by the insights that organize and shape our terrestrial journey. However, although these deductions are, for the most part, based on logic and reason, this presence of mind can touch on the world of abstraction as well. We must concede that thought itself is a non-physical capability and that the thought that is thought does exist, but is difficult to define. Be that as it may, our life-encounters programme our mental outlook to anticipate that a reasonable consequence will evolve from a precipitating cause. If this does not happen, we are puzzled and wonder, 'What went wrong?' We examine the circumstances that could possibly have led to such an unpredictable effect. Throughout our life experience we base everything we do, plan every purposeful move and consideration, on the predictability of the outcome. Our everyday lives are made up of chains of causes and effects that are not self-serving, and the prospect for our tomorrow is determined by the course we set today.

Inherent in this predictability, the presumption that an effect cannot come into being without a cause (and no cause can exist without its effect), is a more significant consideration. If a particular physical composition brings forth a particular intangible performance, we must assume that the two – the physical and the non-physical aspects – are both essential to the particular substance. The flower's assemblage of atoms and molecules cannot exist without the display of its spiritual attributes – the miracles of synthesis and growth. And these non-physical qualities cannot be known or expressed without the participation of the specific material composition. In all its degrees of capacity, Spirit needs the terrestrial substance to disclose its residence. When specified atoms of Energy are gathered together in particular ways, consequent spiritual performances appear. *The material itself is in a constant state of flux*; the constituent atoms are endlessly being introduced and dismissed as the life cycle evolves. But Spirit holds these wondrous particles and their replacements to a purpose and the goal is achieved. As a consequence, the rock, the flower, the bee, and we make our appearance and are thereby enabled to participate in the unfolding of (what we must concede to be) a supreme discipline that has a will of its own.

Is this not quite remarkable? The kingdoms' spiritual capacities remain fixed, although the physical compositions accommodating them are constantly in passage. We, in all stages of our development, from fertilized egg to child to adult, from one generation to the next, reflect human capacities through the employment of the tiniest of particles assembled to make our substance, even though they themselves are with us only for short periods of time. It becomes apparent that Spirit exists by itself, independent of the material forms, and merely uses them to achieve a goal. If this were not so, we would have to question what it is that, in one respect, disciplines the particles to comprise the form, and in another, directs the form toward a maturity and refinement. Certainly the integrity of the atoms is not enhanced along the way, then instilling their own acquired evolution into the forms they take. We have to ask what it is that brings us, with our unalterable but transient particles, through the generations – from denizens of some Paleozoic mire – to galactic wanderers of the universe.

The reciprocal relationship of Spirit to physical matter extends into the quandary concerning the existence of a Creator. As we look around us, it is obvious there is a creation, but how do we know it didn't merely happen? Why couldn't living things evolve from one condition to the next, achieving their heritage through the survival of the fittest and through the processes of natural selection? Through strength or cunning, the survivors would win over the obstacles presented and adapt to the changes inherent in the vitality of the living system. Are we to know only of the effect, and nothing of the cause, because there isn't a cause? Are we, alas, like the others, merely lowly and unwitting participants? Are we whistling in the dark of some age long past, making up this whole Creator-idea so that we can feel better about all the troubles and uncertainties – trusting there is some sense to be made of it all? And does our fear of an unknown, unfathomable, and uncertain future, soothed by the promise of a saving immortality, persuade us to place our trust in, and even base our lives on, covenants that are pledged but cannot be proven? Are there signs available giving reasonable evidence of a Creator who will take care of us with the justness and goodness of His rule?

The answer comes to us when we acknowledge the law that instils the universal patterns and disciplines in the 'worlds' around and within. Strangely enough, by observing the performance of the physical world – the order, the alignments and constraints displayed within and throughout life's structures – we are led to an enlightening disclosure: Life is single and universal! The capability to contemplate so fundamental a truth is a bestowal assigned to our kingdom alone. Our ability to reason not only enables us to examine the mysteries of the physical world, but allows us to acquire knowledge of the non-physical existence as well. How marvellous are our capabilities!

Although the following connections between the physical and the non-physical have already been detailed in Part 1, a review is appropriate here. Evidence of the presence of the *physical existence* we are able to discern comes to us through our sense perception. An awareness of the existence of the *non-physical realities* is revealed through our mental faculties. Our understanding of the existence of these two worlds is substantiated through the use of our human capabilities. This is where our dual nature comes into play.

The Connections

between the **physical** us, and the ***not-so-physical*** us.

The **eye** looks, allowing *sight*, and sight welcomes ***perception***.

The **ear** hears, but *listening* is more, and ***meaning*** is even more.

The **finger** touches, but *feeling* comes forth, and then ***discernment***.

The **tongue** tastes, taste summons *flavor*, and ***distinction*** is born.

The **nose** smells, but *scent* is invited to reveal ***sensitivity***.

We mentally/spiritually process life with our physical tools – our eyes, ears, fingers, and so on. With our ability to attribute non-physical significance to the physical evidences shown, our own spiritual reality comes forward. Therewith, our children can process the attributes of the physical world and find the path to purpose.

It is all so wonderful: the flower grows, the animal roams, and we can muse about the order and the majesty. How glorious! But then the question comes to mind: So what, does it really matter? Yes, it matters. If a wonderful machine hums through its cycle, perfectly synchronized, but accomplishing nothing, where is its significance, where is its counterpart, the effect? Such a machine would be a worthless contraption. So, regarding existence – our world and ourselves – we cannot avoid the question: Is an ultimate purpose being served?

The concept that existence is a hodgepodge conglomeration of miscellaneous shapes and sizes, all gathered together into countless designs and systems, all participating in a random series of events, the consequence of a haphazard evolutionary process, self-driven, without direction, without a primary or sustaining cause or meaningful effect, is ultimately untenable. The lessons gleaned through living our own personal lives and from studying our kingdom's development in history, as well as from observing the processes of life displayed in the other realms, clearly demonstrate that causes and effects, so closely linked that they cannot be considered separate, are inherent attributes of life. One cannot exist without the other. The effect, the happening, comes about through the instrument of some significant and consequential cause; it does not present itself by itself. (Just think. If I had decided not to set out on this writing venture, you might be out taking a stroll in the park.) So, apparently, we must view the evidences displayed, no matter what their aspect, as a series of consequences, each one switching place with the other, the *effect* becoming the *cause* of the next *effect*. It is therefore logical to reason that there is an accompanying primary cause (sorting through all the options, the one most befitting has to be 'Creator') responsible for the overall resultant effect (of course, 'creation'). *If this were not so, the integral parts that constantly and consistently demonstrate this equation would reflect qualities and characteristics not represented in the whole, and this would be unreasonable, inconceivable, and unacceptable.* The ocean cannot contain qualities that are not inherent in the dewdrop; the galaxies' properties are the atom's properties. No, all material and spiritual disclosures are infused with the same intrinsic, immutable correspondence of cause and effect. In their own context, a physical event *and* a mental/spiritual incentive evoke consequences.

Therefore, existence requires not only that the physical *and* the spiritual are two properties of one reality and that each compels the other to become known, but also, throughout the chain of causes and effects, significant purpose is revealed.

And more! In both the material and spiritual realms, a condition is defined by its opposite. We cannot imagine a straight line without having knowledge of one that it crooked. Think of all the comparative counterparts: full and empty, hard and soft, fast and slow, asleep and awake, etc., etc. And 'happiness', as a spiritual condition, is meaningless without our knowing 'unhappiness'. Forgiveness, love, patience, greed, prejudice, awareness – all have their opposites. And the degree is important. We do not designate 'small' as the opposite of 'largest'. 'Smallest' is better. So, in defining the *material, finite, comprehensible*, realities, we are called upon to designate their opposite. It must be *non-material, infinite*, and *incomprehensible*. The word we choose is 'Creator'.

It could be that we ourselves are trying to be too creative when we specifically name and attribute an identity to this Creator/Cause. We give 'Him' a gender, an image we can focus on – even, perhaps, a personality which necessarily must be constrained by our own limited perception. Michelangelo, depicting the Creator bestowing life on His creation, did little to help us understand the mystery of it all. But he did about what we all do. Our vocabularies and portrayals cannot describe the unknowable essence of *any* reality, material or spiritual, and consequently we must rely on our imagery and our superlatives to convey our intent. We are very much like the painting, trying in some way to understand the painter, or like the flower assigned an impossible assignment – to somehow perceive the worlds that surround and sustain. All forms are held to the capacities of their own realm and the kingdoms 'above' are off limits to the ones 'below'. That the flower cannot conceive of our existence does not mean, of course, that we do not exist. Its substance has not been given the capacity to speculate that there exists a greater effulgence than its own – one, even, that can acknowledge its symmetry and fragrance. We are always reminded that Spirit cannot manifest its presence in a degree greater than is potential to the substance reflecting it.

But, because of our enhanced capacities, we human beings actually can 'step outside'of our material composition; we are able to rationalize and analyse regarding our place in the scheme of things. Such capabilities clearly set us apart, but even these extrafordinary tools can bring us only so far in our search to comprehend the essential nature of the kingdom or kingdoms above our own. Our intellectual capacities lead us into areas of awareness approaching the limits of understanding and carry us about as far as we can go.

However, if we (you and I) are open to consider, perhaps allow, or better yet favour, a life force that regulates and coordinates all the systems, an Energy that is 'there' but is beyond understanding, we can have our discussion. Surely this is possible. We will agree that the supremacy of love, imagination, happiness, and countless other abstract considerations, embracing cause and effect, have existence; are we really not able to commend this unknown factor to an *ultimate* supremacy? If we choose our words carefully, is it possible we just might find correspondence and be able to talk about this mysterious force that motivates universally? Even so, most likely we will be discussing the *evidences* and *attributes*, for the realities are beyond us; even the identity of the commonplace stuff – electricity, magnetism and gravity – is hidden. Can we explain the changes that take place inside the cell as the molecules accommodate the processes of living and dying? The secrets of existence are baffling enough without our taking on the Creator.

But it *is* puzzling. We are all willing to accept without question so many mystifying signs, to structure our lives on countless conceptual premises, that it is fair to question why some of us are hesitant to approve consideration of (what in history has been called) the Creator or the Almighty. It would seem, perhaps, that we are dissuaded merely by the name or names we affix, and that within the heart of our innermost being we might privately concede to the existence of such an entity, an entity greater than our own. Be that as it may, if it is truly believed that nothing is hidden, that all the systems are self-motivated or randomly organized, thrown together, a consequence of nothing beyond their own substance, we unfortunately must part company and go our separate ways. I bid you farewell.

Wait a minute! I'm not giving up yet. I can't believe the two of us are this adamant. Let's try switching places. I say to you: 'I think we're making up this whole Creator/God-thing,' and you say, 'Well, if the atoms and molecules are not allowed to assemble everything themselves, or decide when to come on the scene and when to leave, who or what is responsible?' And I say, 'I have no idea, its way beyond me.' And you say, 'Great! Me too; let's give "it" a capital "I"!'

Well, anyway, the premise outlined in these few pages is: Existence is the effect of some absolute and existent but unknown and unknowable Cause (capitalized to designate its primacy), and that the motivating Energy organizing and then using this existence, herein defined as Spirit, is an emanation from this Cause. It follows that this source of life is solitary and separate; 'It' does not enter into its creation, nor does It become a part thereof. Nor does the whole of existence add up to Its identity. Rather, this Supreme Essence is to the spiritual world as the sun is to the physical world, the rays of which energize everything that can receive its light. The sun does not leave its place in the heavens to reside in our world; it is its energy, conveyed through its rays, that infuses vitality into all terrestrial forms.[8] In like manner, the energy of this Supreme Essence emanates in the form of Spirit, awakens its creation, and therewith bestows purpose. In order to focus on this mystery and help define its presence, we have, throughout our history, throughout the world, given identity to and named this source: Brahma, Tao, Yahweh, Ahura Mazda, Mithra, Great Spirit, Jehovah, Elohim, God, Allah, and no doubt many other titles. In this book the name God is used, but only because of my own background. Your choice would be equally appropriate, as long as it serves to define the preeminent Cause.

And Spirit, God's Spirit, the evidence and proof of Its/His existence, *motivates everything*. The pebble (atoms of oxygen, silicon, aluminum, iron, etc.) holds together and performs its function because Spirit is in control. The vegetable can lift these impartial, unassigned, particles from the soil, enhance and elevate their capacities as they metabolize, because Spirit is in command. The animal utilizes these same atoms of energy to express sense perception and instinctual behaviour, because Spirit is at work. We, in our kingdom, use these identical particles to express intellect and free will, because Spirit directs the flow. Thus, through the capacities of physical matter, the Creator/Cause brings forth what we might choose to call the divine intent.

Spirit is eternal. It does not have a beginning or an ending, and, as stated earlier, it and its omnipotent source are separate from creation and *can* exist without such physical evidence. But to be manifested and acknowledged, a material presentation is necessary. The universe is the Creator's playground – His art form. An artist may be an artist without his or her painting, but who would know? In order to demonstrate a creative talent, the artist must put something on the canvas. And if the work is sincere, the qualities revealed on the canvas identify the artist. The signs and authority of the creator of the work are evidenced in the work itself. The universe, creation, with its organization, its economy, and incomprehensible perfection, to the degree that can be expressed and to the degree that can be acknowledged, demonstrates the organization, economy, harmony, and endless perfection of the Creator. It mirrors its maker.

PART THREE

REVELATION – THE DISCLOSURE

Evolution of Purpose

From the beginning that has no beginning, existence has been revealed through the spiritual capacities of the physical kingdoms. Employing the energy inherent in the structure of the atom, this unfolding of life takes place in all the sequential vegetable, animal, and human realms, and it is through these discernible, perceivable, environments that Spirit brings forth the divine purpose. The Creator's universal law, compelling all forms and directing their evolution toward the completion of their life cycles, has orchestrated the development of all physical and spiritual realities. It is through the appearance of the subsequent generations, the ones that gradually are enabled to endure the hazards of survival through their adaptive capabilities, that the Plan is sustained.

Reacting and adjusting to the checks and balances inherent within the equilibrium of our earth's organic system, each form and its parent species evolve, not with willy-nilly abandon, but with direction and discipline. This development is not, however, evoked through deliberate choice. Manifesting enhanced and attuned capacities, the next and new generation unwittingly facilitates the progress. If the form evolves in such a way as to nullify the advance, new forms with adaptable capacities are brought into play. In our own realm, if we, the present generation, do not align to the onward movement, the next and new generation *will comply* and pass us by. In the overall disclosure of life, enhancement and progress, not stagnation and regression, are predetermined factors. The constant refinement of the physical and spiritual capacities manifested through and throughout the different kingdoms attests to the universal nature of the advancement: it does not wait upon our approval.

It is not difficult to acknowledge that our Earth's fragile ecology, with the representation and interaction of the various participants, is no greater a natural phenomenon than is the order presented by the forest pond. Nor is it difficult to extend this equation to the organization of the universe, the employment of the common Energy bonding all forms and systems. However, even though we acknowledge that association abounds, it may be difficult to honour the influence of each shareholder. The incumbency of the mineral to perform its function is easily understood, for all the kingdoms rely on this elemental material for their spiritual display, but the impact of the individual plant, animal, and human being on the whole is open to question. Is the sparrow, or are you and I, connected to the far distant galaxies? Does each form have real and universal significance, not only as a fragment of the whole, but as a fundamental in the ascent of consciousness? Logic supports the argument that creation is single; there is only one existence. It follows that the patterns, degrees, varieties, and intricacies of its functioning are, without exception, unalterably linked. In an organism, as in a machine, the smallest constituent, designed and qualified to fulfil a specific and purposeful function, is relevant to the whole. Logic also supports the premise that the patterns pertinent to the presentation of existence be universally inclusive.

If life appears 'here' on our earth, we must conclude that its essence must be everywhere. In this light, where time and space are not factors, 'every fixed star hath its own planets, and every planet its own creatures'.[9] This means that within all the physical systems incorporated in the organism called creation, the human kingdom or its equivalent is intrinsically implied and potentially present.

On our own heavenly sphere, the scientific community is uncovering the fragmentary evidence of our ancient past. Our old bones and tools link us to pristine beginnings, but in terms of time we are the new kids on the block; our world has been here for a very long time. Considering the age of the celestial systems, particularly and specifically our own with this small earthen dot, civilizations and cultures have developed only quite recently – during the last few hundred thousand or so years. Though it is impossible to describe those ancient Eolithic days, history, if not written, is nevertheless recorded in the buried treasures of our earlier times, and it is logical that these disclosures link us with our *earliest* beginnings. The evidences left by our predecessors, their paintings, implements, and sites, intimate the origin of our evolution, for it is plausible that the gradual progress, from their time to ours, mirrors a *like pattern of development* that took place in the eons before. This supposition is based on the universal law that disciplines the development of life; if the seed holds in its substance the tree with its mature fruit, *a like pattern of fulfilment* is reflected in the evolution of mankind from the seed of our earth. 'Abdu'l-Bahá declares that the comparison can be made because the tree and we are parts of one natural and fixed order. Therefore, we

> . . . will find the smallest atoms in the universal system are similar to the greatest beings of the universe. It is clear that they come into existence from one laboratory of might under one natural system, and one universal law; therefore, they may be compared to one another.[10]

Thus (we may perceive), in the beginning, after its formation from the matter of the universe, before what we call 'life' made its presence known, our world was like a seed or an embryo. Embodied in its substance were the potentials for all the designs and compositions that could (and in some cases, would) gradually and eventually become known. They and their complements lay dormant yet vital within the material of this wondrous earth-pod, 'Mother Earth'. In this pristine quickening environment, over unbroken eons of time, the different and necessary structures that would satisfy life's requirements gradually began to emerge. Compensating for a capacity not hidden in the others, each evolving form enabled the whole organic structure to maintain its balance and move forward. Life was disclosed progressively; first the mineral, presenting a dormant existence apparently without life; then the vegetable realm, verdant, silent, and repetitious; and next the animal, alert and sensitive but constrained by instinctual behaviour. In the womb of this fundamental, incomprehensible, celestial matter, the human kingdom was waiting to reveal itself, and when the sustaining environments were appropriately prepared we gradually began to appear.

When were the first signs visible? It's not fair to ask. When in the growing seed are the evidences of the fruit first made known? Or when, in the development of our own embryos, does our intellectual potential begin to manifest its presence and reality?

The release of this last realm from the chrysalis of the earth marked the beginning of the fulfilment of the Creator's purpose in bringing forth creation – this time on this particular planet – in this obviously perfect residence for life. The details are lost. The early history, locked in stone, is impossible to interpret, but the development of the human kingdom, because it is an integral part of the whole, must have started when everything else started – when the world was first formed, and even earlier. Our realm is instilled in the celestial dust of the universe.

As all matter holds life in its substance, and as life moves toward maturity, constantly adapting to the evolving environments, the shapes and complexities we recognize today undoubtedly had very different beginnings. We, as a kingdom, and as individuals within our kingdom, must have been little more than a potential in those pristine times, manifesting few, if any, signs of a latent humanity. It is interesting to speculate: Our realm, embryonic in the womb of the earth, parallels the development of the child in the womb of the mother. In our kingdom, way in the past, we may have resembled a rather curious and unpromising piscine-like creature. (A fish? Gracious!) However, judgements could not be made, for we were in the middle of our journey, and back then we had to conform, and assume our place in our evolving surroundings; all life emerged from the sea.

Even if we find such an evolutionary sequence unlikely, the illustration is a good one. Addressing the claim of some who are anxious to prove otherwise, it must be stated emphatically that we were always human – or potentially human – a reality other life forms could not claim or rely on even if, way back then, they looked and behaved like us. The simple fact that rudimentary 'gill-slits' appear in the neck tissue of the human embryo gives credence to the nature of our formative beginnings. It is not here proposed that we evolved from the fish. Certainly not! Perhaps it would be helpful to visualize two Paleozoic fish-like creatures swimming together in the same sea. They both look alike and swim alike; who could possibly tell that each one belongs to a different kingdom? Hidden within the one on the left are all the potential qualities of the animal realm, and, no matter how it might evolve in the ages to come, it will never transcend its animal state to become human. Its capacities are locked within the capacities of its substance and the disciplines of its organizing realm. The one on the right is already a human being; it just so happens we stumbled in on its development too early for its potential kingdom qualities to show. No matter how it might develop in the future, it could never be transformed to the animal state; its innate and programmed intellectuality could never be withdrawn from its substance, leaving it to function as an animal creature – perhaps, later on, as a chimpanzee. The spiritual capacities instilled in each realm identify the realm and the only development that can take place is therein defined. One kingdom cannot evolve into another; this could never happen. The mineral could never evolve to the plant; the identity of the plant could never become animal.

Early in our own individual development, when each of us was in our mother's womb, we easily could have been mistaken for a newly formed porpoise, or whatever. But our essentiality was human, not porpoise (which could never develop into a human being even if, somehow, repulsively, its transferred incubation could be sustained). The point is made that we in our realm did not branch off from the animal kingdom somewhere along the way. Some materialists propose there is a missing link bridging the connection between man and the ape. This is a fantasy. The concept that creation was incomplete, imperfect at its inception, that something, not there in the beginning, had to be added later or adjusted to make it right or complete, is not consistent with our perception based on logic and reason. It *is* reasonable to conclude that the mature tree, through all its stages of development, is the consequence of the seed. The earth, in its entirety, is a consequence of the universe. And we human beings, at all times during the stages of our development, were and are the consequence of our world, which brings us back to our being a consequence of the universe. It would be inconsistent to propose that the seed holds in trust every form that is waiting to be revealed except the one that is essential – the fruit with future seeds. The tree is not incomplete or imperfect prior to the emergence of the fruit. It is only reasonable to conclude (and to what avail do we object?) that everything that is here now was always a potentiality, and that our kingdom has always been a part of the realm of the Spirit.

In the process of the Creator bringing forth His creation, at some point along the way we, the *human* beings, structured with potentialities not reflected by or hidden within the other realms, began to sense our identity and awaken to our emerging spirituality. When we had developed mentally to the degree that we could begin to *consider*, to act with intent and react with responsibility to the consequences of our decisions, we entered a new phase of our evolution. No longer were we to depend wholly on the guidance of the universal law, for our coming of age necessitated our *willing* compliance in the divine plan, the plan that stipulates that life must move toward maturity. This time this part of creation must *choose* to adapt to the progress and, with *intent*, discipline its own advancement. This maturing process is similar to the development of the child approaching the age of responsibility. Utilizing what has been instilled and learned in earlier years, after the sheltering environment of the womb and the care of parents and teachers, the charge of accountability becomes unavoidable.

The guidance protecting us as our kingdom approaches its age of maturity has been made available and has been disclosed in a manner appropriate to our present evolved capacities, *in a form that can be understood*. When human beings were developing consciousness, concepts and considerations were, we must presume, revealed by extraordinary individuals who were particularly sensitive to the needs of the hour, attentive to challenges of the time, and aware of the implications implied. With uncommon insight, interpretations were disclosed and resolutions put into practice. A family member or neighbour, *compliant to the Energy flow*, revealed insights which, when shared, enabled the early participants to relate to each other, fashion a tool to scrape the hide or work the soil, and thus move the small community forward. Huddled around the fire at the mouth of the cave, issues were addressed and relevant social and moral considerations were brought to light. Even back then, 'principles' helped the early societies to find their way. The influence of these early teachers, and the precepts that were taught, are lost to history. We have only recently developed language and writing so that our record can be known and appraised. Words, made up of letters strung together and gathered into phrases, convey meanings. We accept this marvellous achievement so casually that we are apt to forget how remarkable it is. A mental/spiritual intent can be expressed merely by a clicking of the tongue, or a scribing of symbols, then processed by the mind through the eyes and ears by way of waves of light and sound, or through Braille, with touch turning into meaning, or signing, with gesture conveying intent. Talk about mysteries!

Recorded history presents sufficient evidence of the influence of social and moral principles as paramount in the development of human progress. Because of their impact, principally because of the civilizations and cultures that consequently were established, we have come to recognize these principles as not only authoritative and responsible for the progress, but have attributed their origin to the Creative Source itself. These principles and teachings have been called the 'Creative Word' because, whether written or spoken, the words themselves, conveying a spiritual intent, open the door to the individual's awakening consciousness, thereby imparting new perceptions and insights relevant to the time. These words and their meanings, which serve specifically to enlighten the *human soul*, are evidence of the presence of Spirit as it works through the capacities of the human realm.

All forms in *all* the kingdoms reflect this presence. The only difference is in the manner of disclosure and the degree of response. Minerals, plants, and animals all take part in their own way. To express the intrinsic purpose of life, the whole of creation is spiritually charged through the varied non-physical capacities of the kingdoms. Here is another comparison. The meanings conveyed through the Creative Word are so powerful that the capacities of the human soul, enabled and brought forth through the employment of commonplace atoms, cannot help but respond. In like manner, the atoms locked within the lower kingdoms' substances are unable to withstand the infusion of spiritual energy that is directed to them, and therewith they manifest cohesion, growth, and sense perception.

The Creative Word not only brings to life the slumbering consciousness of the individual wayfarer, but serves in the larger sense to consolidate isolated and diverse societies to a oneness of purpose that would not have prevailed had these words and their meanings been withheld. It is important to note that the security, integrity, and stability of the community, whether family, clan, state, nation, or inter-nation, and the security, integrity, and stability of the individual within each of these societies, are based on the same spiritual laws. They focus the concerns of the separate and individual participants to serve the welfare of the whole, and progress is achieved.

There is no denying that moral concepts shape human progress. In their history class our children learn about the development of civilizations that have come into being wherever and whenever people were gathered together. History is consistent in supporting the concept that an enabling motivation was responsible for the artistic and innovative record that was left behind. The field trips to the museum bring the ancient relics so close that our youngsters can actually 'feel' the flint chips and the mummy wrappings, and they can understand that those people were as inventive and caring, way back then, as we are today. Returning to the classroom, they will be told that the development of cultures, from those days to these, has been a progressive evolution of social consolidation. However, though this can be a fascinating disclosure, the children will not be told that the Energy at work in the minds and hearts of those early artisans was an evidence of the workings of a wondrous inner Spirit. Our early ancestors obviously were able, but most likely they were compelled to invent such timely tools and express such loving care. They could not help but do what they did.

The evidences of the working of some non-physical force motivating early man, directing his energies to establish the fact that he was human and that he was here, are everywhere apparent. The histories are lost, but there on the plains and plateaus, and in the jungles, and under the sands and beneath the seas, are the evidences of a spiritual excitement leaving little doubt that we human beings have drawn from an Energy source directing us to manifest such creativity. The huge and enigmatic Easter Island monoliths, the imposing Egyptian pyramids which apparently will hold their secrets forever, and the mysterious, primitive Stonehenge with its precise astronomical geometry, were no less remarkable, considering the epochs and eras, than our own achievements are today. Our planet is dotted with evidences of a spiritual incentive compelling us to present astounding examples of ingenuity which were hidden within and then born through the capacities of people – ordinary, wonderful people. (It is interesting to note that long before we were connected by telegraph, radio, or telephone, and although separated by great distances, attuned intellects – guilelessly employing the common Energy – were oftentimes uncovering the same or similar timely discoveries.) We have not told our young students that civilizations are the consequence of the workings of Spirit (or whatever word you are using) as it excites the human soul into action.

The Manifestation

How the spark of thought finds residence in human consciousness has been 'the question' for a very long time. By what process Energy, employing physical matter, gives birth to insight, and how this Energy moves the processes of life forward, remains a mystery. Some of us have concluded that the motivation comes from within, and others are convinced that the instrumentation is bestowed from an outside source. Are we able to find the answer?

It is disconcerting (perhaps *tedious* would be a better choice of word) that our two judgement systems are not disposed to find common ground on which to base their suppositions. The proponents of materialism, those scientists who are holding fast to rigid precepts settled in advance long ago, are ill-prepared to surrender to the evidences of a spiritual presence, even though the Energy that they study, that actually *enables* their study, has in the final analysis only a non-physical identity. Moreover, many of the defenders of religion, perhaps distracted by the redundancies of fixed ceremony and inflexible interpretation also settled in advance way back in history, are unable to surrender to the persuasions of logic and reason, even though order and predictability are inherent in all of life's systems. Apparently we, you and I, must take matters into our own hands, search for truth independently and let the experts go their separate ways.

In our quest to find the common factor which champions and justifies and upholds the *material* **and** the *spiritual*, it will be helpful if we understand the role of intermediary – a bonding agent that connects the two realms. As discussed earlier, all the different kingdoms, mineral, vegetable, animal, and human, are unknown and unknowable without their identifying non-physical qualities – respectively, cohesion, growth, sense perception, and intellect. These attributes do not have substantial presence, as do the forms obliging their appearance. A catalyst or causing agent is needed. Remarkably, this essential enabling factor (which we are calling Energy or Spirit) is not discernible or apprehended until it is reflected as attribute by the physical substance it employs. The attribute itself (cohesion, growth, and so on) is not the Energy. Rather, it is a display or proof of its presence, the effect of its cause. It is in this way, through the instrumentation of substance, that intent and purpose are revealed. Regarding mankind's relationship to the spiritual realm, for free will (*our* spiritual speciality) to be disclosed and aligned with the synthesis of life – so that purpose can be revealed in this greater degree – a bonding agent, a common factor with greater measure of capacity, is required.

As you might surmise, this is the most important part of my book. Inherent in the sincerity of this undertaking is the hopeful hope that the soundness and logic of a proposition can be adequately conveyed through the grasp of a passionate, but ordinary seeker. It is at this point that you and I must be, to some degree, of like mind, for the crux of this proposal rests here. It is obvious that only through independent investigation, pondering in the privacy of one's own inner self, can the evidences of truth be acknowledged. As we struggle to apply the verities of life's oneness to the divisiveness of our merging cultural, racial, and religious backgrounds (factors that once held us together, but now separate), it becomes apparent that these differences are not structured to incorporate naturally. In our search for the oneness of mankind, we must venture outside these restrictive environments.

This being so, 'Abdu'l-Bahá's clarifications regarding the workings of the 'material' and the 'spiritual' are more than interesting concepts; they may, for our time, specifically address our plight and synchronize the course of our journey. His writings are not self-serving; He is not the beneficiary. Rather, the guidance in them aspires to assure and empower each wayfarer embarking on the quest. And, setting partiality aside, the premise is sound and inviting: From the onset of our kingdom's intellectual awakening, human education and progress have relied on the moral precepts and social laws revealed by an unknown number of exceptional individuals, celebrated and documented throughout our history for their role as intermediaries, or 'Manifestations'. Their particular capacity, that of being contiguous to both the *material* and the *spiritual* worlds, connects the human spirit with what is called the Divine Intent. 'Manifestation' is perhaps the better choice of word, for it describes a relationship that not only connects, but one that communicates and exemplifies as well. It follows that the inclusion of the Manifestation and the enlightenment He brings are fundamental and mandatory in the overall presentation of life. Although this might be a conjecture of great significance (i.e., the view that our kingdom's spiritual condition has been awakened and enhanced periodically and progressively through an instrumentality beyond its own capabilities), most of us cannot approve – primarily, for two reasons.

- Many of us, in great numbers, feel that our personal perceptions of honour and truth are inborn in our consciousness and that we are therefore quite sufficient on our own, that we naturally know what is right and good. But our stand is not strengthened by the realization that it is the proclivity, the openness, to these insights that is instilled, not the values themselves. It becomes clear that we must do something with these capacities – direct 'mentality' and 'freedom' toward the purposes for which they were designed. This enlightenment must be learned and then put to use, for it is easy for us to become distracted and set ourselves adrift. Today, the tendency to misdirect this Energy and focus on independence rather than concordance makes it clear that our freedom to go our own way will not discipline our behaviour or consolidate our diversities as adults any more than it did when we were children.

If we still are not convinced of our condition of reliance, there is another consideration we 'materialists' must weigh. If we believe that such an authority as the Creator or Manifestation, with so great an influence, really doesn't exist, and are convinced we are able to design our own rules and establish our own values, we should trace back (to be sure of our certainty) and uncover the source of the principles we intend to use to find our way. If we borrow our justness and our morality from the divine law and claim them as our own, we must concede we are deceiving ourselves and denying the source of our own enlightenment. And if we do set our own rules, we must be prepared for the consequences – for disconnected behaviour, with egocentric goals, places us outside the community. This is self-destructive, for whether our relationship is to family, town, or nation, we are meaningless without one another. Our value becomes apparent only when we contribute to the oneness that defines the entirety. Without guidance and self-discipline, diversity alone cannot provide motivation toward universality, the harmonious condition that defines and consolidates the other realms. It is here proposed that the Energy directing this management is infused in the Creative Word revealed by the intermediary, the Manifestation.

- And if we have taken the other stand, if we are convinced that this management comes from outside our own capabilities but has been bestowed through a single, one-time burst of Energy, there arises another question that is particularly bothersome. To what good fortune do we owe our introduction and enrolment in the best and most befitting social, racial and religious community? How wonderful that we are the right colour and that we find our chance positioning in life closer to the truth than all others. But we must ask: If each of us started our journey embraced by an environment wherein the circumstances of life reflected moral values and social laws similarly structured, but differently derived, would we hold to the same certitude as we now do? Would we feel that others, in far distant lands, were less favoured and, were, in fact, being misled? Here's the persistent nagging question: Could the Energy emanating from all the Manifestations, like the rays of the sun, be universal, boundless, and perpetual, and, because of our isolated beginnings, we are attributing multiplicity to singularity? And could our attraction to the different lamps now serve principally to shield the light from us? If light is light, does it matter if its radiance shines from many sources and in varying degrees? It is acknowledged that the sun bestows its energy gradually as the growing season unfolds. In the spring, the tender shoots would not be able to withstand the direct mid-summer rays necessary for the ripening process.

Let us go on. When revealed by the Manifestation, these Creative Words (i.e., their meanings and significance) become the instrument used by the Creator to develop and guide His human kingdom to the unknowable purposes of the divine plan. They disclose, to our perceptive capacities, the moral and social laws attending to the needs of the present and relating to the promises of the future. This premise requires that we regard the Word – comprising the teachings of all the Manifestations – as equal and true (and thus identical in definition), and that what we perceive as differences and discrepancies are to be attributed to our own lack of understanding, not to any inadequacy of the outpouring.

When the Manifestation appears, His human form is subject to the same constraints as ours, but His human soul loses its personal capacity and identity in the greater infusion of Spirit and is 'consumed' with its effulgent radiance. The Manifestation becomes the perfect exemplification of the sanctified intent. He becomes the perfect human being. *When the atoms of the soil are 'consumed' by the vegetable spirit, they lose their former earthbound capacities in the reality of the flower and become the perfect exemplification of the sanctified intent; they become the flower.* The Manifestation's physical aspect and bearing, together with His contemporary communicative capacities, comprise the perfect vehicle to convey the divine intent to the human-kingdom-consciousness. (You and I would be poor prospects for such an assignment, for even with the purest of motives, sacrificing our egos as best we might, our assessment and perception would still be our own.) We who acknowledge the nature and source of His teachings perceive His personal human life as a sacrifice through which we find our own spiritual salvation. By His own life He discloses how it behoves us to be.

The perfection of the Creator can be reflected only by means of perfect mirrors, ones not sullied or veiled. Whether formed as mineral, plant, or animal, the substances of lower kingdoms respond to the Creator's will, and Spirit is reflected with wonderful clarity. In our human kingdom, because our enlightenment must be processed with understanding, we also need this Energy to be manifested perfectly and directly by an unrestricted exemplification, one not constrained by limited perception, a clear channel that can selflessly disclose the meanings relevant to our capacity, our time, and our need.

The fact that there have been many Mirrors reflecting the same Light does not detract from the singleness of the Light that is reflected. Throughout history, whether human culture bears witness to the influence of the teachings of an unknown, perhaps early, Manifestation, or a well-known Abraham, Zoroaster, Krishna, Buddha, Moses, Christ, or Muhammad, the achievement is the same. Diverse peoples are gathered together and directed to the divine purpose. The fruition of well-defined cultures – Hindu, Buddhist, Jewish, Christian, Muslim – impelled through the progressive nature of the Creative Word, gives credence to each claim.

If we attend more to the particularity and individuality of the Manifestation, if we focus on His personal identity rather than on the oneness of His station and the universal nature of His teachings, we create an obstacle that does not exist. Though He is the way through which the eternal mysteries are made known, the door that opens to disclose the hidden treasure, only His example and His words are the source of our enlightenment. *As beautiful and perfect as the attributes of the flower may be – colour, form, fragrance and all – its essential purpose is to manifest and fulfil its assigned capacity in the organization and presentation of life.* The oneness of existence is confirmed by the participation of each capacity, whether atom, flower, animal, man, or Manifestation. Spirit uses the material substance of every physical form to transmit the Creator's Energy, thus to reveal His purpose.

The residence of Spirit in all the varied kingdoms, enabling them, as restricted and fixed entities, to participate in the fruition of a grand and universal evolution, is inherent in the divine plan, and attests to the unity of existence. The flower and the bee, distinguished and separated by their kingdom's constraints, correlate unwittingly as they process the organic Energy of life. Each fulfils the other. Evidences of this non-physical force are not only discernible, but are commonplace and readily acknowledged. Nevertheless, we hardly pay attention to the miraculous display, taking for granted as normal the spiritual performance constantly emanating from physical matter. Although elusive to explanation and true understanding, we acknowledge this effulgence to be unaffected, direct, and true. 'Abdu'l-Bahá's discussion regarding the availability of knowledge is most enlightening:

> Know that there are two kinds of knowledge: the knowledge of the essence of a thing and the knowledge of its qualities. The essence of a thing is known through its qualities; otherwise, it is unknown and hidden.[11]

This truth leads us to conclude that a contiguous agent is necessary for us to comprehend a reality. Fire is a mystery, but we can know its attributes – heat and light connect us with the essence of fire and reveal its identity. Again, 'Abdu'l-Bahá explains:

> As our knowledge of things, even of created and limited things, is knowledge of their qualities and not of their essence, how is it possible to comprehend in its essence the Divine Reality, which is unlimited?[12]

For this reason (we must respond), the disclosure of the Divine Reality is dependent on the disclosure of the Manifestation. He makes known, through His own knowable attributes and qualities, the unknowable essence of the Creator. The station and capacity of the Maifestation, contiguous to the finite and to the infinite, is a normal property of creation.

The conclusion: The distinct and distinguishing capacities of cohesion, growth, sense perception, and intellect enable existence to manifest, reflect, and bring into being the divine purpose. Regarding mankind's participation, because intellect must find direction, the intermediary (the Manifestation) and the cyclic nature of the message revealed are the connecting and motivating factors in the overall fulfilment of purpose.

If we are concerned that 'our own' Manifestation's integrity is compromised by this premise, we have but to assign His essential identity and supreme authority to all of God's Manifestations, and, as well, allocate all of the Manifestations' essential identities and capacities to His own – the station of the intermediary is inseparable. This simple statement is not flippant or disrespectful – my purpose in writing these pages is to search for the resolution of the problems that divide us. And, of course, these ideas are not my own invention. I am considering them very carefully too. That the contentions between the followers of different doctrines and faiths might be resolved by so simple a premise should most certainly be weighed carefully. However, it would be an error on our part to dismiss a proposal, or reject a verity, because of its lack of complexity.

And the proposal *is* reasonable. If we acknowledge the oneness of the Creator and the oneness of His creation, it may not be difficult to attribute a universal nature to the Energy that connects the two. In the relationship between the Creator and mankind, the messenger and the message is the connection. Today, wherever we are living, we see the gathering of all the cultures with their beliefs and traditions that were periodically instilled in human society when our kingdom was younger. Our outward display of custom and costume, and our various shapes and shades, tell of our isolated beginnings. But the relevance of these differences is being swept away, and we can see clearly that, no matter what Revelation might have guided our progress, we all have been programmed for the oneness of mankind.

****

What would our lives be like without the guidance of the Manifestation? Would we, by ourselves, be able to find the path to purpose? Would not the world and all its inhabitants carry out routines without resolution? Basically, all the forms would borrow their essential atoms from the mineral realm, go through their life/death cycles, and everything would run like clockwork. This would be a humming, but perpetually repetitious world, an existence *leading to nothing in the larger degree.* Thank goodness our participation was planned for and (after some four-and-a-half billion years) we finally have come on the scene. Our intellect actually enables creation to contemplate itself. But this, again, is a trivial pursuit unless there is a further end in view. History describes the progressive development of social order brought into being solely through the influence and instrument of the intermediary and the Law. Lives become focused, principles are infused into hearts and minds, and civilizations are born. But what happens if we fail to respond? Holding fast to outdated systems, covetous of racial and religious heritage, earlier defined and determined for each of us without our consent, we will have to acknowledge that we ourselves are the stumbling blocks in the path of our spiritual advancement and revival. The sudden intrusion of universality into lives and societies unsympathetic to change and fearful of diversity is apparently too bitter a pill to swallow without a fight. We strike out, flailing at the intrusion, viewing with rancour the beauty of our garden.

What happens when we fail to respond?

Enlightenment

When the Manifestation reveals the Creator's intent to the human part of His creation, the entirety of life is, in a sense, reborn. The capacities of every created form are resuscitated when this bestowal is conferred. With the linkage of each species and kind to every other species and kind, renewed and intensified Energy is infused in all the varied participants when the human realm is spiritually set ablaze.

The Energy channelling through the capacities of the mineral, vegetable, and animal kingdoms is universally focused and not diluted by individual abstention; all participants comply. But human response can be fragmented and diluted by individual free will or group resistance, and the universality is blocked. Our kingdom's compliance is necessary so that the universal cycle can be realized, the cycle wherein the capacities of *all the realms* ascend to more expansive spiritual conditions. When our living earth, exemplifying the wholeness and indivisibility of creation, *turns willingly* to its Creator (the entirety championed by our obedience), ultimate purpose is achieved, the cycle of life is completed: matter mirrors its maker. This happens only when mankind freely elects to facilitate its own spiritual awakening.

In the development of our small planet, each participating form, whether assembled as plant, animal, or human, evolves within its realm from one degree of perfection to another, but, as stated earlier, the fruition is not merely and not only physical. As the evolution progresses, the perpetual refinement of the material forms enables Spirit to radiate not only continuously but also with increasing intensity. It is in this regard that we may recognize the evolution of our planet, from the beginning of its life cycle, as an ongoing awakening, a non-physical transformation, wherein spiritual capacities are ever being revealed with escalated and unprecedented potency. Born a silent sphere with unrealized promise, today our earth blossoms with abundant life as Energy motivates countless physical forms in countless spiritual ways in the fulfilment of purpose.

The evolution of all participating forms is achieved through the phenomenon of rebirth: the disclosure of renewed energy by way of the next generation. We might assume that the new offspring would itself instigate the next evolutionary step, but the components – the enabling atoms, molecules, and genes – are not self-motivated, aspiring to stride ahead. Rather, Spirit is constantly charging the passive particles to facilitate the progress. It appears that creation is merely a work zone.

This renewal is relevant to all species and is perpetual. Regarding human development, when we were passing through our adolescent clan-days, the Energy infused (in the form of relevant social and spiritual laws) was a modification of the Energy applicable to our needs today. But the bestowal is identical, and in its embrace is the one precept that is fundamental to all the later stages of our development. We in our kingdom must acknowledge, freely, our spiritual identity and destiny, become aware of the relevance of our lives through the teachings of the Manifestation

and through our willing participation move evolution forward. Because we are restricted by our ties to the physical world, limited by a finite perception of the infinite intent, we cannot otherwise foresee the path leading us to the oneness which is the essence of existence and the purpose of life itself.

Therefore, when considering life as one and all-embracing, the eons of pre-intellectual incubation and the later and gradual emergence of human rationality are parts of the same evolution. In the development of purpose, all aspects and degrees are necessary. However, since the blossoming of mankind's ability to contemplate, the Manifestation and His revelation have been the catalyst bringing forth the maturation of life.

But could there be a flaw in the plan? Although purpose is instilled in the substance of all the realms, in the overall 'ripening' process when compliance and willing obedience become factors, could the whole system become segmented and dysfunctional? It is fair to ask. Could our defection and abstention result in the failure of this planet's inclusion in the ultimate fruition? Is the sowing of life always fruitful or do some of the seeds grow only for a time and then wither away? On this small celestial sphere, could free will abort the whole process? Is it *allowed* that we abstain? In the guise of dispassionate onlookers, are we truly at liberty to upset the plan by merely holding fast to our temporal and secular prizes? What a disheartening thought. Thankfully, there are other factors at work. Even with our wonderful freedom, in the final analysis we are not going to determine very much. The flowering unfolds like this:

Civilizations are established and flourish, but over time the revealed Word, the foundation of society's structure, loses its impact after the goal is achieved. Our allegiance to the principles gives way to a zealous devotion to the **bearer** *of the message and to the* **name** *of the law. We become followers of the lamp rather than the light. Hence, we perceive the new and renewed disclosure to be contrary and competitive. The Revelation, when first proclaimed, might be likened to a pure crystal stream, high on the mountain. As it courses its way through the obstacles in its path, it begins to gather all sorts of extraneous matter until, in the valley, it has become contaminated with all the things that have been added.*

However, though we have muddied the waters, this life-giving stream has instilled enough Energy in our kingdom to bring us to the present time; the divine plan has guided us through the formative physical, societal, and intellectual years. Once residents of a primordial sea, headless and asleep, we now are being alerted to participate in our kingdom's ***global spiritual awakening.***

Is this hard to believe? Well, it is if we let the outward signs distract us, for then we will not be able to distinguish between the death throes of the formative bygone era, and the birth pangs of a new cycle of fulfilment. Many of us are disheartened, believing that there will always be wars and contention between peoples; that we are programmed for strife. But we have never witnessed such an era as this before, and as our spiritual evolution periodically summons new capacities and fresh acuity appropriate to the time, there is, today, reason to be joyful and expectant. There can be no doubt that the new era will bring adjustment and conciliation commensurate to our particular stage of development, for inevitably, as in the past, societal evolution is foreordained, as the fruit is promised in the seed. Having successfully experienced the tribe, clan, and nation, the oneness of mankind is undoubtedly next on our agenda.

In the past, because we have not perceived the continuity, each transition has been beset with difficulties. Adjusting to the evolution, being compelled to give up the tribe to achieve the state, and the state to realize the nation, has been wearisome. And today, our hesitancy to embrace our global neighbour as our friend and the planet as our home is causing grievous repercussions. Nonetheless, as within the other kingdoms, oneness is our destiny. In spite of our wonderful free will, the imperatives of our time are *forcing* us to implement the goals of world peace and environmental stability, overcome the stigma of prejudice and greed, as we become participants in the plan. We are constantly being *compelled*. New perceptions regarding the sacredness of life in all of its aspects disclose the dawning of an era of enlightenment which could not be in evidence or even envisioned earlier, when we were distanced from each other in so many ways. As difficult as the present transition may be, it is clear that only through individual response and submission to the greater cause, putting secular and provincial attachments aside, can we take part in the present and universal resurrection of the human spirit. 'Abdu'l-Bahá emphasizes that peace between nations will not become a reality until unity is established between individuals: 'peace must first be established among individuals, until it leadeth in the end to peace among nations'.[13]

Although our acceptance of the revealed Word and its meanings may be reluctantly acknowledged, or not acknowledged at all, when the Manifestation's season is come and the seed is sown, nothing can divert the development of the 'Tree of Existence'. When the Messenger announces His mission, there is no possibility that creation can remain unaffected. As individuals we may decide to go our own way, but through inspiration and invention we *unconsciously* uncover aptitudes, and *unwittingly* adjust fixed points of view reflecting the new vitality. Without awareness, we change the world in which we live. When the Book is opened and the Word is revealed, every field of endeavour produces marvellous creative achievements. The subtle intrusion of fresh concepts (which come from where?) and expanded understandings (which originate where?) make everyone a participant. These signs are the evidences of a subliminal reaction to the spiritual excitement. Free will is not as powerful as we think it is.

The factors that contributed to our present stage of achievement have come to pass. Principal among these is the development of our kingdom's intellectual capacities which, until our time, were merely potential, held secret within the substance of the early clansman and tribesman, and would not be disclosed until we, their progeny, were to take our turn. This wondrous gift could evolve only through the interaction of people as they met together in the *global* fields of commerce, industry, and science. Science in particular, with its tools and its reliance on logical proofs, was to be the catalyst that would awaken our capacity to reason, and once the door was opened to scientific investigation the myths and superstitions we believed in for so long began to fade away. The resultant grand effulgence of knowledge is now being revealed.

Today, this exhilaration is apparent wherever we look. It is obvious that the course of human affairs is following a path and heading in a direction that we ourselves are powerless to divert – and at a speed beyond comprehension. In the span of a lifetime, everything has changed in astounding ways. At the time I first drafted this book, Barbara's father, Forrest (my father-in-law and friend), was ninety-seven years old. He was born in 1901, the same year Guglielmo Marconi received the first radio message sent from England to Newfoundland. Prior to that time, not much seemed to be going on, compared to today. Forrest recounts the rudimentary happenings surrounding his and his parent's early lives. Do we think that Marconi, and countless others of his time, found this incentive energy slumbering in their inner selves and that they brought it forth by their own will? Or do we acknowledge, as so many of those early inventors themselves did, that a 'supreme Energy' was working through them?

It is relatively easy for inspiration to come to us. In 1844, 24 May to be precise, Samuel F. Morse, tapping out his famous telegraph message 'What hath God wrought!' could hardly have dreamed of the consequences of his discovery. Although it appears that he was not unaware of the source of his inspiration, he most likely was unaware of the significance of that time as he and a host of others opened the door a bit wider. We blithely attribute the scientific revolution to our own investigative, inventive, and intuitive capacities. However, we all experience the excitement of uncovering an idea without particular effort, finding an answer, identifying a truth, not knowing, really, from whence such revelations come. But many of us do know there are *causative factors* on the other side of the physical and mental display, and, without hesitation, acknowledge our dependence on this reality. We try to 'step aside' and find our alignment with what we perceive to be the inscrutable divine will. Through our thoughts and meditations, and our prayers and incantations, we hope to instrument, through our work and service, the purposes of the plan, recognizing that personal interpretations of the divine intent can be flawed by our own fallibility. Therefore, for guidance, we turn away from ourselves to the Manifestation and therewith focus our devotion on the Creator and our energies on the plan. When we recognize the intermediary, lose ourselves in the message and the meanings, we become adaptable to evolution. The *human* being, the 'miraculous cognizant substance', manifests through its awakened capacities the design of its Designer.

Yes, the evolving plan has given us science and the capacities to question and comprehend, and our discoveries certainly have laid bare marvellous mysteries of the physical world; our researchers are as happy and busy as can be. But they shy away from what we are calling the evidences of Spirit, which are right there waiting to be recognized. Since science plays such an important role in our lives, this reticence becomes a major problem, for we have programmed ourselves to believe that 'if science says it is true, it must be so'. Our unfamiliarity with the concept of the *material* and the *spiritual* being parts of one reality continues to be a thorn in the side of knowledge.

The capacity to recognize the residence of truth in all things is a gift given to the generations of our time. The passion to reason and question and process the evidences shown of realities hidden behind the physical and non-physical display has forever been locked in our human substance, but the early seekers did not have, then, today's tools of discovery. Our children do have these tools. To really assist our young people in their quest, the knowledge we share must awaken in them an awareness of the wondrous era they are to bring to pass. We must help them find interests that pertain to their time so that they can direct their energies toward purpose without the waste of boredom, ineptness, and indifference. When their spiritual capacities are so focused, their energies so attuned, their world will be reborn. Their acknowledgement of the oneness of existence will lead to significant perceptions. One in particular will become evident – that, as with any cause and its effect, *there cannot be only one connection between Creator and creation*.

Such insight will lead, ultimately, to the inevitable recognition of *mankind's oneness* and then to *the establishment of world peace*. When the children approach learning with this universal perspective, they will *dismiss preconceptions of all kinds*. Rather, with the assurance that truth is one, they will search and they will filter, and they will uncover the evidences allowed for their time. The oneness will reveal itself in the correspondence of true science and true religion. Gender (determined primarily merely by the presence or absence

> I have yet many things to say unto you but you cannot bear them now. Howbeit when he, the Spirit of truth, is come, he will guide you into all truth, for he shall not speak of himself; but whatsoever he shall hear, that shall he speak; and he will shew you things to come.
>
> *Jesus Christ*[14]
>
> Verily in the histories of the prophets and their people, there is an instructive example unto those who are endued with understanding. The Koran is not a new invented fiction: but a confirmation of those scriptures which have been revealed before it, and a distinct explication of everything necessary, in respect either to faith or practice, and a direction and mercy unto people who believe.
>
> *Muhammad*[15]
>
> In every age I come back
> To deliver the holy,
> To destroy the sin of the sinner,
> To establish righteousness.
>
> *Krishna*[16]

of the Y chromosome in the father's sperm) will be viewed as happenstance. Society worldwide will reflect the equality of men and women. The sacredness of the family, the incumbency of care for the unborn child, and the responsibility of providing safety and education for all children will be considered precious commitments. The integrity and nobility of all life, not just human life, will be self-evident. Religious differences will be wiped away as the children recognize that advancement and enlightenment are mandatory and relevant to all life. In their quest for meaning and purpose, self-giving will clear the way and guide their steps. Marriage will be a lasting commitment as the partners each vow to facilitate the other's achievement of personal and spiritual goals. When we help our children adjust to the requisites of their time, share the assurance of mankind's irrevocable destiny, they will, as cultivators, break the ground for the new habitat for humanity.

The rule of law and the establishment of justice in human society will be acknowledged and defended, for it will be apparent that only through obedience to righteousness and unity of purpose can the individual find security. The perception that nature's law, wherein all life forms find order and correspondence, mirrors the universal divine law, wherewith all forms are directed toward purpose, will be an important consideration. The proposal that a fundamental discipline is in control of and central to both the material and the spiritual aspects of life is worthy of appraisal.

However, for our children to truly participate in this fruition, they must *elect* to implement the progress. They are not too young to understand that merely to submit to the plan, to be used and moved about, degrades their station; the minerals, plants, and animals are utilized in this way. Once our young people understand the importance of their time, the incumbency of their mission, and are assured of their competence, they will permit themselves to be the instruments of universal peace. We must not underestimate the power of the human spirit as our children focus its Energy. Mirroring the image of the Creator, they will, with intent, facilitate the progress and instrument the plan. Their lives will become noble as they 'walk the mystic way with practical feet'.

The world mirrors our own condition. The family is a small town, the town a small nation. More and more of us are seeing past the signs and are beginning to recognize the real cause of our dismay. Violence, hate, and greed are gradually being diagnosed as symptoms of a deep-seated, world-encompassing, spiritual disorder. Terror invades all cities and nations. In our neighbourhoods, as the killing and the mayhem escalate (imposed with casual abandon but apparently with design and intent), many of us are ready to consider any proposal to alleviate the pain and secure the safety of our children. Many of us are taking the big step and then standing firm against the invasion of our moral/spiritual integrity by the forces of materialism and separatism, for we see human values being eaten away by these insidious foes. We are convinced that our kingdom's infatuation with the *physical* and its defection from the *spiritual*, as well as our allegiance to unlimited independence and our rejection of willing correspondence, are bringing their own retribution, and have determined that the correction lies in our own resolve. We are not without a clue; the symptoms identify the illness. Divorcing ourselves from the divine law simply does not work.

When science appeared, a whole segment of seekers detached itself from tradition and set out to discover the residence of truth. Their mission, to intellectually uncover the source of life, was initially eased by technology, but later compromised as research uncovered mysteries beyond comprehension. The goal to fathom the essence of reality remains a dream. And the world of religion, when structured by multiple and unwavering doctrines and immobilized by ancient traditions, cannot reach out and grow and, through its own summoning capacities, quicken and therewith marshal the amalgamation of mankind with the universal standard of truth.

'Abdu'l-Bahá affirms that the quest for truth is an individual undertaking not to be constrained by the perceptions of the past or the trends of the day. The inner core of our humanity attributes to each of us the capacity to understand. The oneness of which He speaks will be disclosed as we alert this capability and ascribe a spiritual identity to all phenomena, to the nature of existence itself, and particularly to the power and place of the human spirit as it relates to every living form. Our human material/ spiritual nature demands that we bring into play a harmonious postulate to validate our search, for, if our spirits are to soar in this day, it is necessary that our material and spiritual wings be equally strong. The time is right for the reappraisal of reality. Today, as the presentation of life reveals itself to our intellectual capacities, we must encourage the children to examine anew the true nature of their humanity and the real identity of their surroundings. Then the assignment of the material world to the station of servitude to the ultimate purpose of Spirit will become clear. They will understand that science without spirituality leads to materialism without conscience and, as well, consequence without purpose; and that spirituality without science presents blind belief and useless superstition.

That we happen to have a role to play at this particular time is the scary part of this whole scenario. Obviously people, *human spirit people*, have been conceived through, born into, and assigned a physical environment within which to work since the beginning of it all, since we emerged from the earth's womb. But we can't imagine ourselves way back in those initiatory times, or even later on when we were chasing after some mammoth mammoth or fending off some formidable foe. We can only place ourselves in the here and now, the era for which all who came on the scene earlier were being used to prepare the way. Can we imagine how our early ancestors might have longed for this moment, in what high regard they would have esteemed our time and task, could they have known? Those waiting, lingering at the mouth of the cave, who were 'moved' to set out in search of the tribe, had their assignment. We have ours. This is why the ones now on stage, young and old alike, must play the role that is programmed. This time we are not playing the part of an 'extra', holding a spear or shield or waving a banner, preparing the way for the principal players waiting off stage. This time we have the lead role, and the oneness of existence is waiting on our compliance. And, of course, we must 'live' the part assigned. Going through the motions and reciting the words isn't enough.

Universal Cycles

Within the structures of life, although there is constant change there are laws that do not change. The fact that change is constant and inevitable and universal is, in fact, a law that does not change. As discussed earlier, all living forms evolve from a beginning to an end and, through the process, achieve 'enlightenment' and maturity. This development is called the life cycle. It is like a metamorphosis. The elemental particles, which serve the purposes of Spirit as it directs the substance through its cyclic phases of life, trade places with one another as they and their replacements facilitate the progress.

The cycles disciplining the organization of life are invariably inclusive; all systems mirror this universal law. Within the incredibly small atom, the electrons whirl around the nucleus at a seemingly impossible speed, billions of trips in a millionth of a second, each cycle a consummating and fulfilling of purpose. And up the scale, throbbing with life and chock full of atoms in the form of molecules, in the form of flowers and chipmunks and you and me, the cells are realizing, through their life cycles, their ultimate purpose – the bringing forth of new cells. Even the seed within each species realizes its objective with the eventual reappearance of its own seed. Inherent in all minerals, plants, animals, and human beings resides the *original* and *undiminished* spiritual vitality that carries the evolution forward. None of the kingdom's Energy 'wears out'.

The cycle of life, which universally touches all forms, is experienced not only through the maturing process of the individual participants, but also through the maturing process of the kingdom embracing the participants. The development of the horse from conception, to foal, to adult, and the evolution of the horse within the species, from the 11-inch high *Eohippus* ('Dawn Horse', 50,000,000 years ago), to the 40-inch high *Merrychippus* (20,000,000 years ago), to the 60-inch high thoroughbred of today, reflect the dual relevancy of this law. We as individuals change and evolve, from a fertilized egg held in our mother's womb, to an awakening child, to a mature human being, in just a matter of minutes (34,000,000, more or less). And the same metamorphosis is taking place in our kingdom as we, ages ago, evolved through the same process from perhaps a simple (but complex) Archaeozoic organic conglomeration, to perhaps a fish-like design, to the beautiful shape embodying us today – some, obviously, with nicer shape than others. Our realm and we, held in the pristine substance of our respective wombs, have evolved together through our particular life cycles.

Whenever and wherever life is presented, it is necessary that its function be started, move through its cycle, and finish at its starting point. To achieve purpose, every form, system and kind participates in this remarkable process. The cycle of the heartbeat, the cyclic flow of breath and blood, the mundane procedures of chewing and swallowing, moving the eyes to the right or to the left – every function involves the beginning and the ending of a returning orbit. The cycle of the second, minute, day and year, the recurring springtime, the returning tide, every tap of the finger, every flutter of the butterfly's wing, is sustained by this universal law – from the smallest and simplest, to the largest and most complex. In this regard, so that the life cycle of the living universe can go through *its* course, accomplish *its* purpose, and start over again, an eventual contraction is implied as the myriad celestial systems dilate and escalate from each other. It would appear the universe is taking a deep breath or winking an eye.

Included in this grand display is the completion of the universal cycle of enlightenment wherewith the consummation of ultimate purpose is achieved. The rhythmic appearance of the Manifestation and the instilling of the Word awaken the unrealized capacities of the human spirit, and the vibrant spiritual springtime comes into being. The vitality of this invigorating rebirth ever infuses the *original* and *undiminished* spiritual energy into our realm, and the fruition becomes a reality.

However, the growing season is only half of the life cycle, for after the midpoint the display of Energy diminishes and then fades away. Then the divine seed is sown again. The reflection of perfection is the goal and this potential abides within the capacities of all human societies. From family to clan, the organization of the expanded social structure and the perfection of its functioning was the purpose implied in the divine revelation of an earlier time. In its degree of social, spiritual, and intellectual development, it was perfect. And so it was with the later divine outpourings, which brought forth the tribe and nation. As perfection is relative and not absolute, the establishment of one culture, with the appropriate degree of maturity achieved, becomes the immaturity and imperfection of the subsequent one. Now we are ready, developmentally, for the establishment of the oneness of mankind with all the ensuing consequences that are implied. 'Abdu'l-Bahá's enlightening commentary on universal cycles is worthy of thought, for it brings into context not only the material and the spiritual aspects of existence, but gives insight to the *ultimate* fulfilment of purpose:

Each one of the luminous bodies in this limitless firmament has a cycle of revolution which is of a different duration, and every one revolves in its own orbit, and again begins a new cycle. So the earth, every three hundred and sixty-five days, five hours, forty-eight minutes and a fraction, completes a revolution; and then it begins a new cycle – that is to say, the first cycle is again renewed. In the same way, for the whole universe, whether for the heavens or for men, there are cycles of great events, of important facts and occurrences. When a cycle is ended, a new cycle begins; and the old one, on account of the great events which take place, is completely forgotten, and not a trace or record of it will remain. As you see, we have no records of twenty thousand years ago, although we have before proved by argument that life on this earth is very ancient. It is not one hundred thousand, or two hundred thousand, or one million or two million years old; it is very ancient, and the ancient records and traces are entirely obliterated.

Each of the Divine Manifestations has likewise a cycle, and during the cycle His laws and commandments prevail and are performed. When His cycle is completed by the appearance of a new Manifestation, a new cycle begins. In this way cycles begin, end and are renewed, until a universal cycle is completed in the world, when important events and great occurrences will take place which entirely efface every trace and every record of the past; then a new universal cycle begins in the world, for this universe has no beginning,[17]

PART FOUR

WHAT *CAN* WE TEACH THE CHILDREN?

A Weight of Responsibility

The idea that the essence of life is exclusively spiritual, that all existence is made up of and controlled by an incomprehensible non-physical Energy, and that all the kingdoms process this vitality to their capacities and to their purposes, is not a customary consideration. Although we human beings exclusively particularize this Energy to discipline our thoughts and organize our lives, we hardly acknowledge its existence. In the course of the day, many of us are not comfortable talking about so-called spiritual things.

Perhaps for this reason, and because it presumes to allude to religion, such considerations are deemed inappropriate subject matter for our children in the classroom. We can all understand why it would be unfair to teach, as a verity, doctrine, particularly a particular doctrine, in the public schools. School is the place where children learn *how* to think – not *what* to think. However, though today's curriculum uses facts and figures to train their minds to process information, it also provides the learning environment wherein each child could and should have the opportunity to discover insights and aptitudes that are hidden within. And these are spiritual matters.

Our fear of tainting the minds of our young people with concepts and beliefs that might be false concepts and foolish beliefs is very real and justified. Our youngsters are so precious: just look at their faces, and just feel the wonder of their promise. However, they know nothing until we older folks share the key to understanding by sanctioning their quest to ask their questions, search for answers, and then find knowledge. They *will* find knowledge, for their investigation will be governed by rational interpretation. If we adults were to switch places with our children, we would not want to be indoctrinated with ideas that might later diminish or even prevent the brilliance of truth from radiating through the windows of our understanding. Nevertheless, what kind of insight are we giving our children that will assure them of the availability of a *meaningful* life and a *purposeful* life if we are, perhaps, unduly careful in monitoring the information that will enable them to make up their own minds and find their own way? In the classroom, they need not be bothered with dogmas and creeds, but can we imagine when they set out for school, their lunch boxes full of sushi, kumquats, pastrami or peanut-butter sandwiches but they themselves lacking acquired knowledge, how anxious they must be to know what life is all about? What is it that makes it work? What bonds the atoms together? What compels the rocks, the flowers, the chipmunks, and themselves to unwittingly correspond? And the children no doubt wonder, 'How can it be that we can wonder?' In the schools we have undertaken the awesome responsibility of educating our children, but because of our fear of religion, we bar the door to their freedom to investigate and question whether or not there isn't something more to life than facts and figures.

Certainly we will not be indoctrinating our young people with concepts and beliefs by exposing them to the non-physical facts of life and to the evolutionary patterns of history. And certainly we will not be asking our students to believe as others have believed by imparting the knowledge that others did have and do have beliefs. We must be careful that our youngsters are not deprived of the knowledge that concepts, strange and wonderful, are part of the human experience – and certainly not only what we have come to accept as religious ideas. Concepts of every kind imaginable, the consequence of the exercising of our spiritual capabilities, flow endlessly from and through human consciousness. The Energy emanating is basic, constant, and accessible, and when our children's capacities are alerted and aligned, they will direct their cerebral atoms and molecules to tap into the flow and bring forth a new world.

This renewed society will not be like the one the children are presently confronted with and conditioned to – an outdated pyramid structure where the 'best' are at the top and the rest are assembled in diminishing degrees of importance below. Children, even the very young ones, should know that life is exciting, that there is a search waiting, and there are prizes to be won. And, lo and behold, each one wins, there are no exceptions! Each child will become aware of self-worth. Aptitudes, specialized by individuality, will become the source of inspiration and invention. Attentiveness and relevance will access introduction to *all the worlds of existence*. Each child will channel Energy differently, and when the intent is sincere and freely expressed, predictability and sameness will be impossible. And yes, there will be only winners – no losers. Competition will be replaced by each child's readiness to help others achieve goals that cannot possibly be his or her own, goals that are attributable and available only to one's own individual particularity. Harmony and correspondence will rule the day. Love, the wondrous innate affinity holding life together, will flow naturally through our children. They will gradually understand why they should have compassion for all souls, residing by circumstance in forms not chosen, and they will love without discrimination even those who do not appear to be lovable. Behaviour toward others in anticipation of an equal return will be replaced by the desire to 'do better unto others than you would have them do unto you'. The consequences will be reciprocal. The new education will introduce such perception.

It is obvious that we do not discourage children in their endeavours to unravel the mysteries of science and to connect with the material world. However, we do the best we can to isolate and even insulate them from an exploration into the nature of the non-physical aspects of this incredible journey. As the children course their way through life, they will, but only with our guidance, *be born again* with the realization that they are a part of something greater. Realization, itself, is a spiritual experience. The children will know that their longing to fit, intellectually and spiritually, into the encompassing organic system is natural and necessary and of great consequence. So why is this wondrous pursuit off limits, especially when we realize that the children themselves, the ones who can actually do the searching and contemplate the findings, are not in any sense of the word *physical* beings? Let's face it: their enabling atoms, in the form of flesh and bone, lack essential substance and fall into the category of intangibility and abstraction. Our children must understand that, as they sit *physically* in the classroom, they are processing the lessons *spiritually* (the mind being the instrument of the soul), and that they will shape their lives with the knowledge learned. The secrets that lie hidden in the physical world and in the spiritual world will be touched on experimentally as they course their way through this terrestrial experience.

There can be no doubt that our youngster's intellectual energies have been directed primarily toward the fulfilment of materialistic goals. However, this sort of achievement is proving to be an unavailing victory when it leads merely to personal aggrandizement and alienated behaviour. Such orientation manifests itself in many ways, but principally in the concept that material gain has something to do with success, and this is expanded to include the view that this measure of attainment is to be sanctioned by the subjugation of others. This perception, considered normal and even necessary by many of us, is not compatible with the principle of oneness. We can understand that the cave dweller was not prepared to reason with his neighbour as to who was more deserving of the cave, and as there had to be a resolution, the one who had the fewer lumps was the one who moved in. But this is no longer appropriate behaviour for our children, or for us.

Today, the endorsement of competition directed toward the domination of an individual, group, or nation over another, betrays our affirmations of brotherly love and erodes the foundation on which we base our humanity. We teach our children to be competitive, to measure their own capacities and accomplishments against the performance of others. This concept of a single standard, against which each individual's capacities must be measured, contradicts our understanding of the sacredness of each child's physical and spiritual bestowal. In this last regard, we must remember that Spirit within each child is perfect and the same. Their individual constraints enter the picture, initially merely through the unforeseeable consequences of conception, the meeting of the components of egg and sperm, and later through life's ensuing vicissitudes. It is obvious that the children's happenstance physical compositions, with commensurate attending spiritual potentialities, have little to do with their *real* identities. As essentially spiritual beings, they are sound and whole, no matter what. Even though their materiality places limitations on their performance, their spiritual 'substance' is essence-mixed with the energies of the universe.

How the *spiritual* can be manifested through the *material* is a mystery. However, working with latent and inscrutable potentialities, instilled when each child is conceived and therewith presented to the worlds of being, becomes her and his terrestrial assignment. The fruition has started. What manner of significant consequence could possibly come forth from such an assortment of atoms as those assembled over there, looking in the window of the donut shop, or these, gathered together, seated, trying to make meanings appear from his word processor? (Can't be sure of the answer to this one.) This is why our children must understand that those of us who are presented with a difficult physical or mental disability, or even a nettlesome personality, are nonetheless spiritually intact. Through the consequence of circumstances beyond our control, our particular assignment and journey are to be especially arduous. However, though heredity and other contingencies might present the human spirit with unusual challenges, oftentimes rewarding and extraordinary qualities of Spirit (perhaps freed of distraction) are nevertheless revealed in surprising degrees and wonderful ways.

Be that as it may, it will become clear that such individuals are in danger of losing the purpose of their lives if they are exiled from the oneness and find they must deal with discrimination and prejudice as well. These abuses bring hurt to the spiritual condition of both parties and of course the entire community is affected. Realizing this, the children will also understand that those individuals whose atoms and molecules are so arranged as to present a most advantageous opportunity to reflect beneficence have the awesome responsibility to be not wasteful of their own special gifts. If we, as teachers, 'indoctrinate' our little ones with essential truths such as these, they will ultimately be able to direct their own progress and seek, with open hearts, the residence of harmony in all things. In their quest for truth distractions will be put aside as they screen opportunities and face challenges. When they meet together in the classroom, colour, race, heritage, and creed as well as physical and/or intellectual differences will be dismissed as accidental happenstance that will not deter their passage into the awesome condition of oneness.

Helping our children to find their place and purpose is the agenda. Deciding on the curriculum, as difficult as this might be, will be the easiest part of the job. As we assist them in their quest for purpose, there is one obstacle that is much more troublesome, for it involves us older folks whose capacities are not so malleable as the children's – our dispositions were formed and set earlier when present-day demands were not relevant. Nevertheless, today, parents and teachers are being called upon to adapt to transitions that until our time were spread over centuries and even epochs. Ours is the generation that must bring the eras together, bridge the social, cultural, and religious gaps so that our children will find their individual lives meaningful as they join the world community. For this reason our responsibility to our children is an extraordinary one.

Preparing the children to meet the new world will be successful only if we ourselves are free to assume such a task. Presenting our inflexible ethnic prejudices and partisan religious convictions as models of attitude that will enable our children to participate in the dawning of universality is unrealistic and unfair.

If we face ourselves, assay our lives, and find that our contributions to society in general and to the children's lives in particular are not directly beneficial, we have a decision to make. If we are knowingly involved in work or other activities that do not support or enhance the dignity of all mankind – particularly the sanctity of the developing children – we must find other occupations. Sharing as we do the one human spirit, we must be careful that we are not the cause of hurt to any maturing soul, for this is where the essence and the core of our humanity lie. If we harm another soul, it is to be considered the greatest and most unbearable offence. 'Abdu'l-Bahá states that, in the days to come, to those so enlightened, the *awareness* of an abuse committed will, itself, become one's punishment.[18]

The children look up from their desks and see the teacher. It is understood that they are the learners, and the teacher is the teacher. Rightly, they have expectations; they are waiting for enlightenment. How can the capacities of the children be ignited if their essential reality is kept secret? Can concerns of the Spirit be introduced to their awakening consciousness without our teaching a specific religious doctrine? Let us hope so, for there is much at stake.

As the children become acquainted with their own spiritual identity and the non-physical nature of their surroundings, they will develop and mature without repression. Their capacities and aptitudes will be free to mirror the Energy that universally permeates life. In the classroom, religion will be treated as a subject. Its influence in the unfolding of history – the part it has played and presently plays in the lives of the peoples of the world – will be part of the school curriculum. There will be nothing to fear, for faith and belief will not be avowed or disavowed; but they will be acknowledged. Of course, the children should know why the postulates of religion are not included in this learning environment. They should rightly know why it *should not* and *cannot* be taught in the public schools. There are obvious reasons, such as which religion should be the one chosen, and, as there are many doctrines of each religion, which one would suffice? But these are not the deepest issues. The reason religion is not for the classroom is because true belief, as the Buddha said, comes to the wayfarer through individual certainty.

> Believe nothing, O monks, merely because you have been told it . . . or because it is traditional, or because you yourselves have imagined it. Do not believe what your teacher tells you merely out of respect for the teacher. But whatsoever, after due examination and analysis, you find to be conducive to the good, the benefit, the welfare of all things – that doctrine believe and cling to, and take it as your guide.[19]

Independent investigation of the evidences of truth is the precious and sole responsibility of the mindful seeker. This is a private path that is directed by one's own conscience and defined by one's particular capacity relative to understanding. Because of immaturity, youngsters are not ready to assume such responsibility. And, of course, the teacher would be able to impart only and merely her or his own personal perception and interpretation of what, in this regard, constitutes truth. Obviously such a bias could have nothing to do with the children and *their* perception. It is difficult enough for us adults to find our way. In our search for truth, we might least expect to find it in the multiplicity of unwavering doctrines. It is only reasonable to acknowledge that we are all responsible to ourselves for our decisions, and that we would not want to deprive our children of this priceless obligation. It must follow that to accept as truth the word of another wayfarer, learned or not, is to automatically forfeit understanding and responsibility, for if we do not know of ourselves, we cannot truly and with assurance be certain of our conviction. The classroom is a wonderful place to learn, to touch on knowledge by solving problems, asking questions, and searching for answers, but we mustn't determine for the children what is to be believed or what is true. Even in science, with all its facts and logic, theories are only pencilled in.

However, the following is true: today's technology spreads before us a sumptuous feast, and our students are the ones who can see and touch on the mysteries of life as they have never been seen and touched on before. What an exciting time to pop in on our kingdom's progress! As Mom and Dad wind their way through the maze at the Mall, does their tiny tot, looking up at us from his stroller, have answers waiting behind those beautiful eyes? In the schoolroom, will it be that fourth-grader, over there, studying her biology lesson, who will discover that some non-physical Energy is at work within little Skip, the classes' pet salamander? Will she, with her deductive reasoning, conclude that the little amphibian wouldn't be available for study were it not for the spiritual energies hiding within each of its enabling atoms? In the larger sense, will she venture to name this Force, and acknowledge that *It* is the factor that disciplines each atom to comply with the requirements of the particular kingdom that is using it – in this instance, assembling little Skip and holding him together? Will our young student discover that the study itself would not take place if her own atoms were not so perfectly arranged that she could concentrate, store the knowledge, and draw from its resources to write her paper – with, of course, the help of a whole assortment of atoms in the shape of a pencil?

And over there by the window, will that 12-year-old psychologist, lost in thought, come upon the insight that the workings of the mind, the non-physical performance of intellect and behaviour – even the thought that is thought – cannot possibly be disclosed without his cerebral atoms being spiritually charged to perform these specific functions? And in the larger sense, will he venture to attribute an identity to this Energy, recognizing its independence of the form it uses? All that is left, aside from the continuing investigation into the physical world that surrounds us and the spiritual attributes that define its inner workings, is the search for a perspective that will unite the two. Relegating the material and the spiritual to separate and opposing fields of inquiry has, until now, distorted our perception of what the term 'truth' implies. Perhaps our two young students' paths will someday meet and their conclusions will help everybody understand the oneness of it all. We casually say, 'The Creator works in mysterious ways', but certainly practical ways will not be brushed aside. The Energy flows and is manifested throughout the plan, and there can be no doubt that the capacities of our two budding researchers, and the little fellow cruising the Mall, will help provide the means so that the Creator's will can be done. How else could the divine intent come about?

Looking around the classroom, the children can see the new world being born. Seated over there, and over there, are the doctors, architects, technicians, artists, teachers, and caregivers of tomorrow. They are the replacements for those who are so occupied in the world outside. In the years to come, when all the children from around the globe meet together in the fields of commerce, medicine, and law, they will bring their backgrounds – their colours, customs, and beliefs – with them, and they will be the activists for their time.

But before they all meet in society's colourful casserole, it is important that each child, in each classroom, in each town of each country, be introduced to the differences out there. Not so much the shades and nationalities, for these have not been kept secret, but the beliefs and traditions, which have long been perceived as private and shrouded and considered as never to be considered.

But why not, what could be the harm? One background is as different from another as another is from the one. It doesn't matter that we, their teachers, subscribe or not to this philosophy or that. It does not matter that these ideas or those are foreign to our way of thinking or that this persuasion or that practice is, in our view, right or wrong, good or bad. What matters is that belief and tradition are a part of our present and a part of our past and have always been instrumental in holding diverse and isolated peoples together. The picture of history that we paint for our children should place moral concepts and spiritual laws in the centre of the composition. It really matters that people did, and do, believe.

Our students would find it interesting if they could investigate the ancient philosophies responsible for the various cultures that have played a part in their evolution. Their history books describe the civilizations that developed, but there is little chance that our children's present-day intergalactic perceptions could relate to the dawning consciousness of the primordial tribesman. And then, too, there is little chance that much of the initial intent is to be evidenced in the mysterious cave paintings or deciphered from the honoured burial sites, or the charred ashes of the sacrifice.

I mentioned earlier that the 'Manifestation' part of my book presented a problem – for me. I was apprehensive about my capability to adequately set forth the premise, and I considered putting it aside, being content only with a discussion of the non-physical nature of physical matter. But we are concerned about the education of our children. The whole of this little book is directed ultimately to the needs of our young people. Teaching them about the physical and the non-physical aspects of life, as important as these are, cannot be complete without including the nature of their own spiritual capacities, and the transforming process that is necessary for their development and fruition.

How the Manifestation, the intermediary, plays a part in the children's lives is essential information, absolutely vital if they are to place themselves in the linkage connecting and coordinating all life – bringing it together and to a purpose. As stated earlier, the particles destined to serve the minerals, plants, animals, and human beings are passive, waiting to be charged by the intermediate Energy so that cohesion, growth, sense perception, and intellect can be brought into play. To the limits that comprehension allows, the presence and nature of the essence within is revealed through attributes that can be known. The degree of Energy tolerated links the material substance to the spiritual performance. In the human realm, the same universal intermediary (Spirit, if you like) awakens our substance to the condition of awareness. To circumvent the importance to the processes of life of this connecting factor (in all its degrees of disclosure) because of persistent protests by rock-hard members of the scientific community, or others who are perhaps doctrinally disenchanted, would leave my book with its complete story untold.

However, circumstances are changing. Though programmed by a long-standing tradition that automatically dismisses a kindly view of a so-called spiritual reality, these traditional and adamant outlooks are giving way to more lenient deliberations. As the laboratories reveal new discoveries beyond reasonable interpretation – mystifying patterns of behaviour in the most secret and elemental structures – insightful biologists, physicists, and genetic researchers are beginning to write their papers with more and more reference to the non-physical energies controlling particle behaviour. And others, who consign spirituality less to doctrine and more to universal approbation, are searching and testing, seeking the evidences of truth, unlabelled and undefined.

This is good news for our children. Admitting the non-physical realities into the frame of our acceptance will enable us, as teachers, to broaden the scope of inquiry made available to our young people. When we become accustomed to the relevance of Energy to matter, the concept of an intermediary impelled to reveal insights that when addressed become the source of human awareness and progress, will not be perceived as myth or magic. The chasm dividing materiality and spirituality will be bridged with the understanding that truth is one. Perhaps because beliefs in the supernatural distinguished our formative-age mentality, some of us feel it is time to move on, that this kind of reliance should be set aside, retired, that our modern ways render such conjectures obsolete. But this is surprising, for in our own era of logic and reason our lives are constantly being shaped and directed by inspired thoughts that somehow just come to us, like magic. Our minds are constantly bringing forth particularized impulses that not only define our individuality and make our presence known, but are relevant to our time. Why not an intermediary whose thoughts and insights are not *His* own and come from 'God knows where'?

If we continue to draw a line between factual knowledge and perceptive reasoning we will continue to distort our children's assessment of their world and themselves. If the purpose of life, particularly an individual life, is not addressed, they most likely will conclude that it is pointless to survive in a meaningless world. The imposed isolation from thoughtful considerations (not their truth or falseness, but merely their availability) implies a bias that rests on the shoulders of the teaching community. This neglect must be considered an abuse, for the rights of our young people are being denied. We must ask ourselves, 'Is it enough to teach young seekers that this physical world and the worlds beyond merely exist, or would it better to permit them to consider any reasonable probability?'

Our little ones have no idea what truth is all about. Passing over the scope of inquiry accessible will not prepare our children to consider options as they develop toward maturity. If we are not candid and forthright regarding the choices that might lead them to answers, we are not fulfilling our responsibility in preparing them to cope with the obligations and opportunities that lie ahead. In this regard, the children should know not only of the non-physical Energy that is instilled in physical matter – they can call it what they like – but they should understand how they relate to this Energy and how it enables them to fit, intellectually, into the ordered patterns of life. The quickened child will ask questions, and be encouraged to ask lots of questions. Most likely, the teacher will be challenged with: 'Why is it important that I memorize and figure?' Or, 'Who cares when Vasco da Gama sailed to wherever? Will such information bring me happiness, or help me find my way?' Or, 'Why do I have to compete with runners who are faster than I am?' Or, 'What makes the flowers grow?'

As the children set out in search of purpose, we, their teachers, must be predisposed to acknowledge their individuality. Each child has hidden talents and interests that must be uncovered. But this in itself is not enough. Even in the primary grades, the children are not too young to begin to use their awakening consciousness as an instrument, so that concepts and consequences can gradually be dealt with as they approach the age of responsibility. Encouraging them to think and memorize and figure may be challenge enough for the teacher, but the underlying factor to which all these mental disciplines relate, and on which they depend, must also be addressed.

And yes, the children will pass us by. Freed of attachment to outdated systems, they will merge into the oneness and therein find peace, place, and purpose. Their world – and ours – will be reborn.

PART FIVE

THE QUEST

Considering our history, it is amazing that we are here, that we can look back and measure our progress. Many species have fallen by the wayside. We might stand proud and claim to be survivors, but the notion that we are being watched over escapes no one. From cave to nation, we have come a long, tortuous way and now, because we can see our direction and foresee our goal, it is clear that we have one more obstacle to overcome. The unity of existence cannot become a reality until the oneness of mankind is achieved. As we hold fast to our perceived differences, struggle to function with divisive and outdated rules, it appears we are still too rigidly focused to single out the common threads tying us together. Structured so similarly, we acknowledge mutual concerns, share 'human feelings' and profess our need to live in harmony, but our inflexible doctrines and the myriad redundancies we attach to the same verities linger as stumbling blocks. The forms and rituals we thought would enhance and glorify fundamental truths now serve principally to obscure the singleness of humanity's spiritual reality and destiny.

Today, as we merge together in the global fields of commerce, industry, scientific research and all, we see our governments *being forced* to find better ways of resolving political and economic differences. Our representatives meet around the conference table, propose resolutions, and sign agreements, but as citizens of the world, where are *we* to find the guiding principles that will erase *our* prejudices and bring us together? As creation is the commitment of the Creator, manifesting His reliability in the impartial bestowal of His Energy, providing every kingdom and kind with its appropriate apportionment, we, the species that can seek, we, the ones who can acknowledge and respond, must be attentive to our time. The laws connecting us exclusively to the tribe and nation have served their purpose and are no longer relevant – even though some of us still clamour; our fitful behaviour still holds us at bay. Our oneness requires universal precepts that will embrace us all and address our common and universal social and spiritual goals. Since we are not able to direct our own progress and invent our own rules, we must prepare for the renewal that comes from beyond ourselves. The signs and warnings that invariably bring to a close a bygone era are everywhere apparent. Principally, the breaking down of the divine law is sapping our energy, crippling our resolve, and, at this particular time, delaying the establishment of universal peace. Interpreting the sovereignty of the Word to accommodate our separate, perhaps worldly, even self-serving, agendas is inflicting its own retribution, for hate, envy, greed and indifference have replaced love, compassion and care. It is at such an hour as this, when the tide is low, that we must be expectant, alert, and accessible, for the cycle is at its midpoint.

So! Let's get ready, unpack, put aside all those things we really do not need and set out on our search together.

> We are about to go on a journey into an 'underground' world, the world of meanings hidden beneath the appearances of things, the world of symbols where everything is significant, where everything speaks to those who can hear.
>
> *Peul oral tradition*

Independent Investigation

The ideas expressed in this small book are not contemporary ones. As I write (in Spring 2006), they are forerunner ideas, sown for our time but not fully grown. They are just beginning to peek above the surface. They were planted when Bahá'u'lláh announced His mission way back in the middle eighteen hundreds (1863). However, considering the scale of time, this is really not so long ago.

The big picture, the biggest one we are now able to paint, places us in the last microsecond of history. (Even the current moment has hardly a life span, for by the time we process its increment, it is already a part of the past.) However, we might venture to say that we are the forerunners of the time scale, for you and I are capsules of all that has come before us. Every event and every thought that has found expression has networked through the ages to reside in our being. Therefore, we have a connection with *every thing* that has happened, and there can be no doubt that those future generations, way off in distance and far away in time, will be influenced by our contribution and they will remember us for the part we played.

Certainly we can acknowledge the momentous changes that have taken place since that proclamation in the nineteenth century. Adding them up and assessing their impact on society, we might best describe their appearance as forecasts of the dawning of a new era. Apparently Bahá'u'lláh's teachings and principles are so momentous that the state of the world is to be changed as never before. Can the present and sudden impetus be the consequence of any other single initiative, especially as human *progress* until this time has crept along for centuries with progress as such hardly in evidence? In particular, the discoveries of science, energized through the infusion and release of unprecedented Energy, have triggered world-embracing interaction and advancement. Over a period of some three hundred years, the hidden knowledge was suddenly made knowable. Bahá'u'lláh's Declaration in 1863, as attested by His own words* is easily acknowledged as the focal point of this progressive outpouring.

1700 Theory of probability	Bernoulli
1718 Mercury thermometer	Fahrenheit
1769 Steam engine	Watt
1780 Law of combustion	Lavouster
1783 Hot air balloon	Montgolfier
1790 Contact electricity	Galvani
1804 Locomotive	Trevethik
1807 Steamship	Fulton
1829 Locomotive (first practical)	Stephenson
1831 Law of electrical induction	Faraday

* "Soon will the present-day order be rolled up, and a new one spread out in its stead" (*Gleanings* IV, p.7, para.2).

1830s Analytical engine design	Babbage
1843 Telegraph	Morse
1839 Photography	Dauguerre
1861 Telephone	Bell, Reis
**1863 Declaration*	*Bahá'u'lláh*
1867 Dynamite	Nobel
1869 Periodic system of elements	Mendeleyev
1876 4-cycle gas engine	Otto
1873 Electromagnetic theory	Maxwell
1877 Phonograph, electrical	Edison
1979 Light bulb	Edison
1979 Electrical locomotive	Siemens
1885 Motor car	Benz, Daimler
1888 Electromagnetic waves	Hertz
1892 Alternating-current generator	Tesla
1985 Cinematography	Lumiere
1895 X-rays	Roentgen
1897 Wireless	Marconi
1898 Radium	Marie Curie
1900 Quantum theory	Planck
1903 Motorized airplane	Wright Brothers
1905 Theory of relativity	Einstein
1913 Atomic structure	Bohr

Each of these instruments was to serve the needs, not of isolated tribal communities, or even nationalistic goals, but rather the purposes inherent in the fundamental structuring of an emerging world civilization, toward which and for which Bahá'u'lláh's revitalizing teachings were revealed. Going back a few generations, we were connected to the land, not to ideas. And, away back, before technology was to even hint at its presence, one common day and one ordinary decade doggedly followed another, hunkered down under the weight of repetition; no excitement of discovery, no inkling of what was to come. And now the world is exploding!

The relationship of the smallest to the largest taxes our comprehension; the atom to the universe boggles the mind, even though we know that the universe is made up of atoms. The linkage of the microsecond to eternity presents a blurred vision, even though we know that microseconds make up eternity. However, when we, you and I, attempt to place ourselves in the current state of affairs – in the context of present time and history – we will most likely agree that science gives us better tools to work with than religion does. Science has the upper hand in explaining the secrets, because facts and figures give us a palpable measure. Rational considerations, particularly those regarding cause and effect, ultimately commend a theory of evolution and place the claims of religion in a defensive mode, for with the overall temporal display the interpretations of scripture can lead to all sorts of conclusions. And when it comes to the evocation of awe, evolution does not take a back seat, for its workings are no less a mystery.

Putting the above aside, more recent documented history gives us a clear view of how fast and how far we have come. With a little research, we can easily list the changes and refinements that now define our own and our children's lives compared with those that describe our parents' and grandparents' lives. Just a moment ago, on the time scale, life was very different.

How an individual's awakening comes about is a mystery. How is it that one person finds interest in history and another in music or accounting? The fact that we are all so different, no matter what our upbringing, education included, proves we are individuals right from the start. Apparently, the way we are put together will determine who and what we are to be. But who we are to be does not become apparent until we find interests and choose choices. We hold dear the freedom to make these choices, but we are not comfortable or effective unless we select the right ones and then do something.

However, not just through childhood, but throughout our lives, much of our time is spent reacting to others' needs. From little tikes on up, we are constrained by parents, teachers, employers,

Time Scale

ERA	YEARS AGO	PERIOD		EPOCH	CHARACTERIZED BY
Archeozoic	5,000,000,000-1,500,000,000				earth's crust formed; unicellular organisms; earliest known life
Proterozoic	1,500,000,000-600,000,000				bacteria, algae, and fungi; primitive multicellular organisms
Paleozoic	600,000,000-500,000,000	Cambrian			marine invertebrates
	500,000,000-440,000,000	Ordovician			conodonts, ostracods, algae, and seaweeds
	440,000,000-400,000,000	Silurian			air-breathing animals
	400,000,000-350,000,000	Devonian			dominance of fishes; advent of amphibians and ammonites
	350,000,000-300,000,000	Mississippian	Carboniferous		increase of land areas; primitive ammonites; development of winged insects
	300,000,000-270,000,000	Pennsylvanian			warm climates; swampy lands; development of large reptiles and insects
	270,000,000-220,000,000	Permian			many reptiles
Mesozoic	220,000,000-180,000,000	Triassic			volcanic activity; marine reptiles, dinosaurs
	180,000,000-135,000,000	Jurassic			dinosaurs, conifers
	135,000,000-70,000,000	Cretaceous			extinction of giant reptiles; advent of modern insects; flowering plants
Cenozoic	70,000,000-60,000,000	Paleogene	Tertiary	Paleocene	advent of birds, mammals
	60,000,000-40,000,000			Eocene	presence of modern mammals
	40,000,000-25,000,000			Oligocene	saber-toothed cats
	25,000,000-10,000,000	Neocene		Miocene	grazing mammals
	10,000,000-1,000,000			Pliocene	growth of mountains; increase in size and numbers of mammals; gradual cooling of climate
	1,000,000-10,000	Quaternary		Pleistocene	widespread glacial ice
	10,000-present			Recent	development of man

10,000 years ago = 3,650,000 days = 87,600,000 hours = 5,256,000,000 minutes = 315,360,000,000 seconds

2,000 years ago = 730,000 days = 17,520,000 hours = 1,051,200,000 minutes = 63,072,000,000 seconds

1,000 years ago = 36,500 days = 8,760,000 hours = 525,600,000 minutes = 31,536,000,000 seconds

100 years ago = 365,000 days = 876,000 hours = 52,560,000 minutes = 3,153,600,000 seconds

10 years ago = 3,650 days = 87,600 hours = 5,256,000 minutes = 315,360,000 seconds

1 year ago = 365 days = 8,760 hours = 525,600 minutes = 31,536,000 seconds

1 month ago = 30+ days = 720 hours = 43,200 minutes = 2,592,000 seconds

7 days ago – Last week = 168 hours = 10,080 minutes = 604,800 seconds

Yesterday, at this time – 24 hours ago = 1,440 minutes = 86,400 seconds

An hour ago – 60 minutes = 3,600 seconds

A minute ago – 60 seconds

• Right now, this second, as we are processing this *word*.

friends, and, once in a blue moon, by spouses, who have included us in their own agendas. Therefore, in the midst of all this to-do, it is nonetheless of vital importance that we set aside time to weigh the options and pursue our dreams. The challenge to keep the goal in sight is critical, for it could be that, because of the intertwining of life, the equilibrium of the *whole* requires that Energy be reflected by its parts in necessary and determined measure. As with the forest pond, the varying capacities of each of its participants must be displayed. In the wonderful mutuality of life, the myriad capacities, instilled without 'anyone's' approval, complement one another. When all life's realms (i.e., minerals, plants, animals and people) reflect the common Energy in their allotted ways and degrees, the oneness of existence becomes a reality. To sustain the balance, our particularized contribution is *mandatory*.

It is interesting to speculate: can we, you and I, be certain that our participation in the movement forward is generated through our willing determination and adaptability, or is it because our instilled capabilities, not chosen, are needed in the mix, and we then unwittingly fill what would be a gap? If this is so, existence counts on our contribution – cannot foresee our abstention and then compensate for that lesser degree of Energy until it turns up missing. Therefore, if we find that we are bored with our work, find it unrewarding, it is probably because we are doing the wrong work – work that should be another person's opportunity and, in a sense, responsibility. (We would have to search for a long time to find a bored, dysfunctional, unhappy bee.) This is also the reason children should not be required to measure up to predetermined and impersonal standards of excellence, for their capabilities are particularized. And this is why we are happiest when we are free to make these choices. It is disconcerting to acknowledge how little time we have to just think about things and wonder about things and to speculate about where, in the blending, we are needed. Plodding along, passive and indifferent, robs the whole of life of a contribution and capacity on which it depends. It is for this reason that meditation and prayer are important, for they provide a detached environment enabling us to become a part of the greater cause and link with the greater realm.

Greater realm? What greater realm? Well, this is not an everyday consideration (though it should be), but bear with me for the moment. From little people, just born, through our later years, we are surrounded by the endless display of physical sights and sounds. The material world is everywhere. Unless we are informed, the other non-physical domain will be unknown. Usually we consider spiritual matters to be religious in nature, and for many of us who do not subscribe to sect or doctrine, the reality of a spiritual world gets little press. But reason ultimately commends the existence of the non-physical realities; we know that existence is more that just a physical phenomena, because it behaves. And those of us who do align ourselves with religion and the environment of church or synagogue or mosque or temple find, perhaps, little that connects us with an expanded concept of spirituality; to be spiritual, we must go to church, et cetera.

****

Truth is not fully accessible, and those of us who are interested in looking for its signs will hover and circle around its essence, hopefully coming closer, ever closer. We must be courageous and step outside the norm, because the ongoing dissension between sincere followers of religion and thoughtful disciples of science presents a challenge rightly assigned, perhaps, to the impartial observer and independent thinker. In the face of so much controversy, the quest for the residence of truth and knowledge is a justifiable cause. Search implies investigation and, as our two schools of thought are locked in their ancient and opposing traditions, the answers may not be found within their current hypotheses. And certainly today, unity in any regard is an exemplary goal. If truth is one, then adjustments are necessary in the doctrines of both disciplines. This does not mean we must retreat from the concerted effort and set out on our own. Coordination is the hallmark of life; none of us accomplishes anything alone, and knowledge is built on the verities of the past. It would make sense to examine again the established premise and give it a friendly twist – decant it and therewith see the evidences in a new light. The problem that arises today is that most of us are put on the defensive: we must choose sides and pledge allegiance to one but not to the other of the two systems that define reality. But existence, single and complete, governed by Energy, unknowable but true, necessitates a genuine and concerted response.

****

Throughout creation, atoms are the principal players. But they can't do very much by themselves. Thankfully, each one is so enamoured of its similarly inclined neighbour that they hold on to each other for dear life. And we cannot help but marvel at their versatility. Grains of sand or stellar galaxies, wow, what a romance! And when they find themselves gathered thus in more inclusive assemblies, and they are now a petunia, or a hummingbird, or a happy child, a child who will aspire after truth, they might wonder how it could be that they are given so little credit in facilitating the lifting-up process. How could they possibly know that, to become a part of something greater they must give up their solitude and independence – and not even dare to dream of freedom?

How these different minuscule particles evoke such remarkable and diversified effects is the challenge confronting our children today. Unburdened by old-world attachments, their quest will be successful because they will be using the mind tools of reason and logic to process the unprecedented flow of scientific disclosure. The hopes and dreams of the early seekers will at last be realized through the capacities of their heirs. The knowledge of the oneness of the material and spiritual aspects of life is but a click away.

Such questions were the talk of the town some little time ago. People were excited about Darwin's theory and Huxley's declaration. Today science has advanced its speculations and, though they are slightly more than mind-boggling, we hardly blink an eye. Perhaps we think the theories are too complicated, or we *really are* too occupied with the routines of the day to give them the time of day. But what about interesting? Are not the findings fascinating? Our ambivalence might be attributed also to the layman's loss of faith that there truly are answers to perplexing questions. And our reticence to react is not exclusive to scientific proposals.

For the most part, most of us sit and listen to others. By the thousands (hundreds of thousands, millions?), we watch the track meet, the rock concert, the tennis match, the religious revival, the flight to the moon – all performed by a selected few. How is it that *they* are the talented ones? Dance? 'I don't think so; I've got two left feet.' Hmm; well, it could be that *they* were encouraged, when they were little, to think and imagine and dream and wonder and hope and trust, and then, as a consequence, gradually discover a special interest, a fascination that they could not hold back. Most of us, the onlookers, may have been apt students, able to understand the questions and come up with the right answers, but oftentimes we were bored with the repetition, and restless with the humdrumness of it all – 'Who cares when Galileo was born?' Somehow it didn't dawn on us that all that memorizing and figuring were the *tools* for learning; knowledge would come later. What a rude awakening when we entered first grade and all the stories and fairy tales and fantasies were left back home on the bookshelf in our bedrooms as we turned our attention to the real world of facts and figures. The wonderful sparkle in our child-eyes dimmed as we were turned into grist for conformity's mill. Our spark was not fanned into flame. If we were given a failing grade, our energized particularity, not attuned to a predetermined and impersonal standard of excellence, was given a knockout blow and we decided, inwardly perhaps, that it is best to sit on the sidelines and watch the procession pass by. Let the smart guys do it.

Well, what about church or synagogue or mosque or temple: is this the place where we find the excitement of discovery? Well, let's see. As we sit listening, just for fun let's venture to glance to our right or to our left and then study our faces. Happy? On fire? Afraid of the fire? Why so sombre? is spirituality such a solemn business?

Do we show the thrill of understanding, which we cannot keep to ourselves? I asked a pastor friend, 'Has anyone come up to you after the service to share an inspired thought or proffer a different interpretation?' He said, 'Regrettably, no.'

So now, we sit on the porch swing and watch the passing parade.

The hollow asylum to which we have retreated, that *allows* us to merely look and hear, is truly a disquieting residence, apparently inuring us to shock but rendering us passive in the wake of the surge of unprecedented ideas and expanded understandings. The dilemma, a general quietude in the face of new challenges, may be simply the consequence of the primary education to which we of the present generations were subjected. Or perhaps, along the way, we placed our trust in powerful people, mostly self-proclaimed, who told us that they knew better that we did. As youngsters, we were taught to listen and to 'not ask so many questions', but now that we are older and more self-confident we certainly should have the courage to question those in command. 'Does that really make any sense to you? Where did you get such an idea?'

As an example, the religions of the world are anticipating the fulfilment of the promise of all ages, that a great world-teacher will appear '. . .in the fullness of time, to carry on their mission and bring it to fruition'. When Bahá'u'lláh announced to the world that He was indeed the Promised One, just a handful of folk responded. Whether His claim is true or not, one would think there would have been an overwhelming reaction, a joyous celebration or a most serious and thorough investigation. Yes? No. Rather: 'Ho-hum, you don't say.' Some years ago, a neighbour couple took Barbara and me, as newcomers to Brown County, for a ride through the hills to see the countryside. I don't remember how the subject came up; we must have been talking about religion, and (I'll call him) Bill said that he and (I'll name her) Dorothy believed that Christ would soon return, suddenly, unannounced – perhaps in the next moment. That His head would come down in the clouds, and he and Dorothy would instantly be lifted up, and they would join with some few others to form His body. And they would go to Heaven. Assuming that Barb and I would not be making the trip with them, I remarked, sitting on the driver's passenger side, 'I had best be ready to take the wheel.' I didn't ask, 'With all that you know about clouds and sky, does that *really* make sense to you?'

The Pearl of Knowledge

The early clansmen and tribesmen trudged through life unaware that they were forerunners, laying the groundwork, building the infrastructure for the oneness of mankind. Most likely it all started when we were minding our own business, warming up a tasty mammoth cutlet or fashioning a pointed stick when another ruffian and his family ventured on the scene. As you know by now, if I had been the cook or carpenter I would have hit the bloke with my basting spoon and bid him farewell. But of course, in due course, their son Ebb and our daughter Flow found they were hopelessly in love, and they, it turns out, gave birth to the tribe. They could not have known that instilled in their own substance was the gift future generations (but not ours?) would treasure and for which they would offer prayers of thanksgiving. We, the beneficiaries, are still hesitant to open and embrace this precious inheritance. Are independent investigation and the search for truth – the pearl of knowledge – so awesome a responsibility that we feel unworthy of such a bestowal? Are the assertions of the strong amongst us still so compelling that we are willing to step back, and not question their assumed authority? Do we follow because we truly believe?

The sanction to ask questions and weigh answers, along with an abiding interest in the workings of nature, will prepare children (soon to be adults) to examine and choose options and seek relevance in all things. The study of nature's law is important because we have come up through the ranks and are, even with our free will, a part of the order. And independent investigation is important because it will unlock the mysteries and bring meaning to the children's lives. They will gradually understand that they are preparing themselves to be responsible for their own spiritual condition. It will open windows and doors, and the light of understanding will radiate from their souls. The search for truth, free of attachment to outdated beliefs and systems, will ultimately light up our world

At the time of this writing, this greater realm, the province of Spirit, is believed by many of us to be non-existent. A good number of scientists have held fast to this premise. Programmed by a long-standing tradition that acknowledges the existence only of the 'material' and the 'physical', many are hesitant to explore the cause of all these puzzling effects; they study and scrutinize, hoping to find, somewhere hidden *within the effects*, the ultimate cause. And there are other practical thinkers who are so fearful of religion, or of even an acknowledgment of the possibility of a greater realm beyond the observable one, that they have taken an unwavering stand against anything that carries its 'taint'. But they both get low marks when called upon to explain the natural flow of consequences. Every effect necessarily must have a cause, be it a quaking volcano or a thoughtful thought. As the enabling atoms and molecules, placed by happenstance in the bowels of the earth (volcano) or in the convoluted folds of the brain (ideas and understanding) are without will, then something – something residing outside their 'substance', something apparently inexplicable – uses them for the desired effects: an intermediary, if you like, which connects them to the greater purpose. The only option available that would help explain this phenomenon is locked in the atoms themselves, but this is not satisfactory. The fact that some of us define this non-physical motivation as 'spiritual' should not cause the materialists to be unduly fretful; they may call 'it' what they like – merely choose another word. To universally explore and embrace such a premise, we have a way to go, it would seem. But insight can come to the open and inquiring mind instantly, and once the investigation is freed of attachment to preconceptions, the unity of existence will be revealed. Perhaps we are waiting for that fourth-grader with his or her burning interest in genetic research or bacteriology to 'discover' that existence manifests itself with the inherent alliance of the material *and* the spiritual.

The catalyst that will bring all this about is remarkably simple. All we have to do is teach little children to ask questions. Ask questions and open the way!

****

Incorporated in the changes that accompany a new era is the inability of society to adapt to transformation without a fight. This rebellion occurs whenever the more prodigious infusion of Energy is released and mankind is directed to a greater degree of maturity. From the family to the nation, we have been guided through the ongoing enhancement of the community, and now we are to be shown the way to a world civilization. The rancour and hate will begin to disappear as we unwittingly adjust to the requisites of the new world order. The constant wars and revolutions that mark our history are the consequence of man's disobedience to the Law, and in this sense he brings the dysfunctionality on himself. Though we have fought tooth and nail to keep our tribe or nation isolated, though we have built up all kinds of walls designed to keep us apart, the fact that we are now adjusting to a global social order proves that we are powerless to prevent the advancement. And this implies that we could have arrived here without all the fuss. Today, holding on to the past, covetous of (mostly religious) tradition, tribes, clans and nations are being thoroughly shaken to free them of the dross of prejudice, and, as well, they are being gathered unwillingly together to address the stigma of isolation. Age-old separate doctrines are struggling to contend with the intrusion and impact of universality.

Is there a chance that any of these doctrines will become the focal point of the new world order? Will they be able to strip themselves of the redundancies and accoutrements that cloud the brilliance of their fundamental truth? Which one shall we choose?

****

The purpose of existence is that it manifests itself with its singleness employing all the varied capacities of the kingdoms. This was not a problem until we human beings decided to grace the amalgamation with intellect. It was then that all our neighbours started to have problems. The wild creatures were overrun; they could not find a safe haven – anywhere! Clouds rained acid, and primaeval forests turned into urban sprawl. The wilderness found itself ignored, sickened, polluted by the consequences of our freedom, and it didn't take long for our planet to manifest the symptoms of a deep-seated disorder. Global warming and natural disasters should not come as a surprise to any of us. We thought our independence was a proof of our superiority and that, somehow, we could impose it without consequences. Now it is snapping at our heels.

The Creator/Cause has to be unhappy with so dysfunctional an effect, not only with our disorientation, but also with our hate and suspicion. Today terror invades every town and nation, and we wonder, 'Where is the Love that gathered us together in the first place?' The atoms and molecules do a better job of holding their neighbours close than we do. Worldwide, we refuse to acknowledge that we are the people of the world. Bahá'u'lláh wrote, 'The earth is one country and mankind its citizens,' and, 'O Son of Spirit! My first counsel is this: Possess a pure, kindly and radiant heart, that thine may be a sovereignty ancient, imperishable and everlasting.'[20]

Not even imagining the possibility that religion has the answer to our problems, we wonder what we can do to reverse the trend and save our planet and ourselves.

Bahá'u'lláh states that religion is the safeguard for humanity. It is the only discipline that will so change and charge the human heart that the individual will surpass himself and become a part of the greater call. If we, as seekers, search for and find spirituality for our own sakes, it is not enough; this is merely a selfish endeavour, bearing no fruit and leading to nothing in the larger degree. Spirituality is a single condition, but it is manifested in restricted degrees. The mineral, plant and animal kingdoms display its presence perfectly. How interesting it is that their powers flow so easily into each other. However, we, in our realm, reflect spirit imperfectly because we, the individual constituents, vary and differ in our ability to individually reflect our kingdom's full potential. The standard of perfection for our kingdom is the Manifestation – the Christ or the Buddha or any of the other founders of the world religions. And the teachings and principles He reveals, structured to consolidate our diversities and then bring forth the Kingdom of God on earth, are not optional, they are inevitable.

All the Prophets communicated this Message to the rulers of their time, but these were too self-occupied to respond. Bahá'u'lláh, while in exile and prison, wrote epistles to the kings and emperors, announcing His mission. He declared that His message to the world was the same message Abraham, and Moses, and Buddha, and Zoroaster, and Christ and Muhammad had brought to the developing human social order. All the lessons, designed to enhance the maturity achieved through the earlier teachings, were to be regarded as chapters of one book. Just a moment ago, the concept of 'the oneness of mankind' could not have been understood by minds adjusting to the requirements of the clan or tribe; this 'education' would come later. Each revelation served to enhance mankind's spiritual development and, through incremental growth, reach its spiritual destiny. Christ taught his disciples to do unto others as you would have them do unto you. This was a fundamental of His revelation. Bahá'u'lláh enhances the Law with the proclamation that we must do better unto others than we would have them do unto us. The consequences will be reciprocal and benefit the whole.

The law of self-abnegation, of surrendering to causes beyond one's self, enrols us in the universal fulfilment of purpose. When we are brought into conformity with the patterns and disciplines of life, we find peace and happiness. Personal salvation takes on a new and greater meaning than the mere assurance that we will live forever, seated at the right hand of God. Personal salvation, in truth, means that we give of ourselves, direct our energy to the benefit of others with whom, perhaps, we have no personal relationship. We love others so much that we are willing, even eager, to give the gift of ourselves. Jesus did this. The consequences will be reciprocal and benefit the whole.

****

Most of the principles of the Bahá'í Faith are now firmly implanted in the consciousness of the world, if not yet in practice. The emerging world community, though struggling to acknowledge the equality of men and women, and still struggling to banish and overcome the stigma of racial, religious and cultural animosity, is nonetheless beginning to recognize the appropriateness and urgency of these goals. But there is one principle that is difficult to convey and equally difficult to understand. It is not because the concept itself is too obscure, but because it is too elemental. Bahá'u'lláh refers to the different founders of the world's religions as Manifestations; They manifest the perfection that mankind aspires to achieve. They are, in a manner of speaking, all Saviours, lifting mankind up from the darkness and dross of materialism into the light of spirituality. As their single purpose is to guide mortal man toward loftier goals, they are to be regarded as identical, equal and true. Bahá'u'lláh states that all the Manifestations are essentially the embodiment of the same and universal Spirit, though their physical attributes and personalities differ. He explains that these holy souls are commissioned to share the bounty of enlightenment commensurate to the capacities to which they are directed and for which they are designed. (Commissioned by whom? None have claimed a personal initiative or motivation.) Thus, there is only one religion, which has been revealed progressively down though the ages, and one Intermediary through whom the meanings are conveyed. This is the principle that is difficult to understand, because today the followers of the religions believe their Manifestation is the only true one, and that His Book is the only source of enlightenment. And this doctrine, in turn, leads to the conviction that the source of all truth is Buddha, not Krishna; Krishna, not Moses; Moses, not Jesus; Jesus, not Muhammad, and so on. Bahá'u'lláh compares the Manifestations to rays of the one sun shining with increasing intensity as the growing season unfolds.

There is something very strange about our relationship to religion. Its purpose is to bring individuals into unity and then focus their collective energy to achieve spiritual goals. We seem to feel that religion belongs to us, that it is ours, rather than the other way around, the Creator's. Religion (Truth) retains its integrity, identity and authority with or without our support. If we choose not to align ourselves with its discipline, we inflict the deprivation only on ourselves. Religion has been the foundation of society for a very long time. Along the way, we, as believers, grace it with our attention only fleetingly.

CONCLUSION

Well, here we are at the end of my book. I delight in your resolve. Normally an artist does not have cause to be a writer, but the perils we face today assign to each of us expanded responsibilities. Considering thoughtful, sound, propositions that address our spiritual depression might even be an obligation. It is becoming obvious that traditional remedial measures are proving to be superficial and ineffective. The loss of conviction that God and His Laws are real and true, and are not to be manipulated, is manifest throughout the world. The claims of materialism, the plague of intolerance, and the grip of isolation are overwhelming, and the consequences of such dysfunctionality cannot but mislead our children. It is for this reason that I put pen to paper. As I stated earlier, the writings of Bahá'u'lláh and the explanations of 'Abdu'l-Bahá (as I understand them) are the basis for this whole dissertation. Obviously only one's own inquiry can establish certitude regarding the validity of any proposal, especially when it encompasses abstruse considerations. Each of us has a heritage that determines our attitudes and channels our insight, but these fortunes are peripheral to our competence, as human beings, to acknowledge evidences of truth.

I cannot help wondering: what would I be like if the circumstances of my life were entirely different? Let me share my fantasy. In the secret realms of everlastingness, a soul-to-be was waiting for assignment and, by happenstance, this elemental entity was to be me. In this flight of fancy, my parents arrange for my habitation and bring me into the world, not in Evanston, Illinois, USA, but rather in a remote valley of Tibet or perhaps Chile. If this were the case, my personal and present world would be very different. My parents would teach the lessons appropriate to our time and place, and I would be impressed with a certain confidence that our way of life, our customs and our beliefs, were quite satisfactory. And indeed they would be, for mankind's progress has been shaped by the evolution of separate societies and the moral laws governing them.

Although my residence in Tibet or Chile or the United States may be fortuitous, I now find I am not only a citizen of my town and country, but that clearly I belong to a single close-knit world community. My children (and grandchildren, if you are as old as I am) are no longer isolated in their national and ethnic identities. Their neighbourhood classrooms mirror the amalgamation blending races and cultures which we older folks, as youngsters, would not have known. Polynesian and Ugandan and Argentinean children are finding that their common kingdom is dressed up in all manner of custom and costume, and though the display is stunning and beautiful, the individuals so attired are basically not different at all. It is obvious that our great need is to find a new and universal spiritual perspective that will, in its all-inclusiveness, not only reflect our diversities but will sustain them. The soil of the human spirit is ready for the oneness of truth to be sown and harvested universally.

We, the educators, must unburden ourselves so that we are free to defend our children. This small book is directed to those parents and the teachers who are on the quest, who are ready to examine and question the relevance of the resolves proposed by government leaders and social psychologists as remedies for our present spiritual dilemma. The incarceration of our children in the inner city is not the problem. It is a symptom of a plight that endless funding for better housing will not alleviate. Sexual misconduct among our young people is symptomatic of an affliction that sex education and the distribution of condoms will not remedy. Nor will the handing out of free hypodermic needles attack the moral plight. The boredom, apathy, and insensitivity; the lack of regard for self, family, and community are signs of the abuse of the human spirit that money and things, however necessary, will not set right. Disregard for law and order, without concern for consequences, is the symptom of a spiritual void which stronger laws and more severe penalties will not allay.

And the hurt is apparent not only in our young. The adult community, again apparently without a sense of connection, is giving mixed signals to our young people with its outward admonitions and its inward coalition with dishonesty, intolerance, and greed. Through advertising and other forms of commercialism we present licentiousness as love, violence as entertainment, and the use of alcohol as innocuous and manageable, when we know better. These, in themselves, are not the problem; they are signs of our spiritual bankruptcy, and they bring into question whether we are competent to shape the spiritual destiny of the innocent and uninformed child. And if we are not, where are we to find the unadorned spirituality so powerful that our hearts and minds will not be able to countervail it? Do we have the courage to put aside the palliative measures and face the cause of our dismay straight on? Are we ready to acknowledge that the problems, not the symptoms, are spiritual in nature; that killing, hate, envy, anger, and immodesty are signs of the state of our spiritual health and that to confront the plight effectively we must be lionhearted and resolute? Ultimately we must resolve into first principles. Legislating to fund better housing, better schools with better education, better laws and enforcement, better everything, while neglecting the basic underlying sickness is proving to be futile.

The remedy outlined in this inquiry is not complicated. The basis of the whole speculation is borrowed from the evidences of order and purpose presented in the natural environments surrounding us. Since we are as connected to the worlds of existence as any of the other realms, and as the great oneness embraces all, the fundamental precept must relate to us as well.

To sum up briefly: *cause* brings forth *effect* employing **Energy**. In the material world this vital, enabling, factor does not have physical properties. It resides outside of the substances it uses, and therefore we designate its nature to be non-physical, recognizing its essential identity to be unknowable and thus an evidence of the presence of a central and fundamental cause. Some choose to name this force 'Spirit' and its source 'Creator'. Thus we say the Creator brings forth His creation with His Spirit. In all the kingdoms, this universal Energy is infused into each participating form, and each responds as its capacity allows; the enabling particles are charged to accommodate cohesion (minerals), growth (plants), instinct (animals), and intellect (us). However, in the human realm, our instilled capacities need to be brought to life – born again. Reason and freedom of choice are not sufficient and fulfilling in themselves; we must manage them in ways that are meaningful, ways that align our energies with the unified purpose toward which creation's unwitting participants are directed. In order to respond to the summons and direct our focus, we initially must acknowledge the Creator as the entity apart from ourselves and the source of the bestowal, and then recognize the contiguous, exemplary capacity of the intermediary as the means through which the bestowal is conveyed. The intermediary is necessary because, in a particular regard, a cause cannot enter the effect – it creates the effect. The sun does not leave its place in the heavens so that life may benefit from its energy. Rather, the connecting capacities of its rays energize all forms in appropriate degrees. Likewise, the Creator does not leave the realms of the infinite to dwell in the province of the finite. Rather, the intermediate capacity of the Manifestation conveys the divine intent.

In both regards, the intermediary is the means linking the cause and the effect.

In the human realm, the one progressive revelation can be likened to the ongoing profluent nature of the education that aspires to guide our children in the schools. The teachers, competent to teach and thoroughly versed in the subject, share their knowledge to the degree suited to the students' capacity to understand. Their training affirms their competence to teach advanced lessons, but this would be inappropriate for those who are just beginning the course; the proficiency of the students necessarily determines the lessons to be assigned and acted upon. Next season a new instructor (no doubt distinguished with particularity) will teach a more advanced course to address and build on the students' achievement. It is acknowledged that the instructor is necessary to assist in making the learning experience more meaningful, through thoughtful interpretations and explanations. In all the classes, the perfecting that takes place is the same; it brings the students from one degree of maturity to the next. The achievement of one grade becomes the starting point for the next. The former lessons are not forgotten but are enhanced to facilitate the progress.

The eternal mysteries instilled in the Creative Word, hidden and waiting for discovery, make up progressive revelation. This vitality is not static but adapts to the developing capacities of the human soul – hence it is called the Creative Word. To be attentive to the premise, we will assign the identity of all the Manifestations to a universal station and their teachings will be regarded as chapters of one book. When the Manifestation states that only through His capacities can the truth be known, He is referring to His station and His role as intermediary, not to His human individuality. His perfection is of the Spirit, not of the body. This is why all the Manifestations present themselves as the sole connection between God and creation, and attest that the message they reveal is one and true. This is why they all claim to be the only way, and warn us against choosing, with our free will, other gods and other paths that are always close by such as worldly attachments and frivolous concerns, designed, it would seem, to distract us. Their message is clear: the material world does not hold the coveted prize. They caution that such trappings, seemingly harmless in themselves, are apt to become addictive and then consequential as we direct the course of our spiritual journey. The consequences of our response are explicitly defined. Nearness to the divine purpose is to be perceived as Heaven, Nirvana, or Happy Hunting Ground. And, so that we might understand, remoteness from this wondrous condition is depicted as Hell, Purgatory, Eternal Death, the Great Abyss. Nearness to the oneness of existence brings fulfilment; separation results in purposelessness and aimless wandering.

In conveying spiritual principles, the Manifestation reveals teachings that inspire the seeker to sacrifice personal independence for a unity deemed to be the goal. **Moral principles**, laying the foundation for all the societies that mark our history and progress (family, clan, state, nation, and inter-nation), and **social laws** designed to change and adapt to the growing needs of the community, have provided signposts and security for the individual wayfarer. These lessons are progressive, but identical. They enable us to develop and adjust to the evolving physical and spiritual environments over which we have no control; social laws leading us out of the cave into the clan and nation; moral laws, attuned to our capacity to understand the meanings of justice and love.

The oneness of existence embraces everything. The Creator, His creation, and Spirit, the connecting factor, comprise the whole. The Spirit part, bestowed with purpose in all forms, is what we might identify in a general way as the 'universal faith' – the surrender of physical matter to the will of the Creator, the sacrifice of limitations to the purposes of universality.

This concept brings into unity the Creator and His creation; the oneness of existence is made apparent, and it also brings into the composition the contentions of materialism and spirituality; the integrity of these two declarations, which give credence to existence, are honoured as parts of one reality. It also brings into focus the progressive nature of revelation that has forever and will forever sustain life as existence serves the Creator's purpose, reflecting His omniscience and will. If, in our traditions and scriptures, we believe that God the Creator has deemed it just to favour a part of His creation and withhold His bestowal from another, we must go to our Books and find the meanings that reveal His steadfast love for each and all. If we have interpreted that we are the chosen few, that 'we are this' and 'they are not', we must look again at the words and find the hidden meanings that reveal our fundamental oneness; a wholeness that cannot function without the participation of the least of us all. When we find in our hearts the desire to truly love each other, to extend this love to all His realms, we will fulfil our kingdom contract. We will then serve to consolidate the oneness of existence with our willing compliance, surrender to the divine Law, turn with devotion to the One who embraces us all, and present to Him the gift of His own creation.

Endnote

I thought you would like to have my mother's recipe for Lace Cookies.

1 cup quick oats
1 egg, well beaten
¼ lb. melted butter
¾ cup sugar
3 tsp. baking powder
1 tsp. vanilla

Butter and flour cookie sheet (Barbara bakes them on baking parchment paper) and space teaspoons of dough far apart, as they will spread flat. Bake at 350°F (180°C) until edges are brown – 8 to 10 minutes. Remove from cookie sheet while still warm.

May Scheffler

Reflections

Pierre Teilhard De Chardin (1881–1955), French ethnologist, anthropologist and priest

Love alone is capable of uniting living beings in such a way as to complete and fulfil them, for it alone takes them and joins them by what is deepest in themselves.[21]

Considered in its full biological reality, love – that is to say, the affinity of being with being – is not peculiar to man. It is a general property of all life and as such it embraces, in its varieties and degrees, all the forms successfully adapted by organized matter . . . And in fact if we look around us at the confluent ascent of consciousness, we see it is not lacking anywhere.[22]

John, Viscount Morley (1838–1923), English statesman

. . . contented acquiescence in the ordering that has come down to us from the past is selfish and anti-social, because amid the ceaseless change that is inevitable in a growing organism, the institutions of the past demand progressive re-adaptations.[23]

Lewis Mumford (1895–), American sociologist and writer

The segregation of the spiritual life from the practical life is a curse that falls impartially on both sides of our existence.[24]

Isaac Newton (1642–1727), English philosopher and mathematician

I seem to have been only like a boy playing on the seashore, and diverting myself in now and then finding a smoother pebble or a prettier shell than ordinary, whilst the great ocean of truth lay all undiscovered before me.[25]

Thomas Paine (1737–1809), American Revolutionary writer and natural philosopher

Infidelity does not consist in believing, or in disbelieving; it consists in professing to believe what he does not believe.[26]

It is certain that, in one point, all the nations of the earth and all the religions agree. All believe in a God. The things in which they disagree are the redundancies annexed to that belief; and therefore, if ever an universal religion should prevail, it will not be by believing any thing new, but in getting rid of the redundancies, and believing as man believed at first.[27]

Joseph Ernst Renan (1823–1892), French philosopher and historian

O God, if there is a God, save my soul, if I have a soul.[28]

John Ruskin (1819–1900), English art historian and educationalist

The first duty of a State is to see that every child born therein shall be well housed, clothed, fed, and educated, till it attain years of discretion.[29]

Abd-ar-Raham (912–961), Caliph of Cordoba

I have now reigned above fifty years in victory and peace, beloved by my subjects, dreaded by my enemies, and respected by my allies. Riches and honours, power and pleasure have waited on my call, nor does any earthly blessing appear to be wanting for my felicity. In this situation, I have diligently numbered my days of pure and genuine happiness, which have fallen to my lot: they amount to fourteen. O man, place not thy confidence in this present world.[30]

Henry Brooks Adams (1838–1918), American historian

We shall some day catch an abstract truth by the tail, and then we shall have our religion and our immortality.[31]

Anonymous

There is something in between physical matter and religion.[32]

Henri L. Bergson (1853–1914), French philosopher and scientist

The present contains nothing more than the past, and what is found in the effect was already in the cause.[33]

Leo Nicholaevich Tolstoy (1828–1910) Russian writer

Man has received direct from God only one instrument wherewith to know himself and to know his relationship to the universe – he has no other – and that instrument is reason.[34]

Albert Schweitzer (1875–1965), German physician, philosopher and musician

One truth stands firm. All that happens in world history rests on something spiritual. If the spiritual is strong, it creates world history. If it is weak, it suffers world history.[35]

By having reverence for life, we enter into a spiritual relation with the world.[36]

Louis D. Brandeis (1856–1911), US Supreme Court Associate Justice

If we would be guided by the light of reason, we must let our minds be bold.[37]

Edmund Burke (1729–1797), Irish-born Whig politician and man of letters

There is but one law for all, namely, that law which governs all law – the law of our Creator, the law of humanity, justice, equity; the law of nature and of nations.[38]

Confucius (551–410 BCE), Chinese philosopher

Do to every man as thou would'st have him do to thee; and do not unto another what thou would'st not have him do to thee.[39]

Peter Cooper (1791–1883), American industrialist and philanthropist

Let our schools teach the nobility of labour, and the beauty of human service, but the superstitions of the past – never.[40]

Albert Einstein (1897–1955) American (German-born) theoretical physicist, originator of the theory of relativity

Something deeply hidden had to be behind things.[41]

Nationalism is an infantile sickness. It is the measles of the human race.[42]

Science without religion is lame, religion without science is blind.[43]

Francisco Ferrer y Guardia (1859–1909), Spanish educationalist and freethinker

The school imprisons children physically, intellectually, and morally, in order to direct the development of their faculties in the paths desired. It deprives them of contact with nature, in order to model them after its own pattern.[44]

Edwin Markham (1852–1940), American poet

By a divine paradox, wherever there is one slave there are two. So in the wonderful reciprocities of being, we can never reach the higher levels until all our fellows ascend with us.[45]

John Stuart Mill (1806–1873), English political economist and philosopher

> A person may cause evil to others not only by his actions but by his inaction, and in either case he is justly accountable to them for the injury.[46]

Anonymous

> There is a principle which is a bar against all information, which is proof against all arguments and which cannot fail to keep man in everlasting ignorance . . . that principle is contempt prior to investigation.[47]

O SON OF MAN!

Veiled in My immemorial being and in the ancient eternity of My essence, I knew My love for thee; therefore I created thee, have engraved on thee Mine image and revealed to thee My Beauty.

O SON OF MAN!

I loved thy creation, hence I created thee. Wherefore, do thou love Me, that I may name thy name and fill thy soul with the spirit of life.

O SON OF MAN!

If thou lovest Me, turn away from thyself; and if thou seekest My pleasure, regard not thine own; that thou mayest die in Me and I may eternally live in thee.

Bahá'u'lláh[48]

Bibliography

'Abdu'l-Bahá. *Selections from the Writings of 'Abdu'l-Bahá*. Haifa: Bahá'í World Centre, 1978.

—. *Some Answered Questions*. Wilmette, ILL.: Baha'í Publishing Trust, rev.ed. 1984.

Atlantic Monthly, The (New York), November 1958.

Bahá'u'lláh. *Gleanings from the Writings of Bahá'u'lláh*. Wilmette, ILL.: Baha'í Publishing Trust, 2nd ed. 1982.

—. *Hidden Words of Bahá'u'lláh*. Wilmette, ILL.: Bahá'í Publishing Trust, 1990.

—. *The Summons of Bahá'u'lláh*. Haifa: Bahá'í World Centre, 2002.

Bergson, Henri L. *L'evolution créative*. (Paris, 1907). Trans. Arthur Mitchell. New York: Henry Holt & Co., 1911.

The Bhagavad-Gita, Song of God. Trans. Swami Prabavananda and Christopher Isherwood. Hollywood, CA: The March Rodd Company, 1941; RP Vedanta.

Bond, E.A. (ed.). *Speeches . . . in the Trial of Warren Hastings* (1859).

Brewster, David. *Memoirs of the Life, Writings, and Discoveries of Sir Isaac Newton* (1855).

Dhammapada. *Wisdom of the Buddha: The Unabridged Dhammapada*. Trans. F. Max Müller (1900). New York: Dover, 2000.

Dukas, H., Hoffmann, B. *Albert Einstein, the Human Side*, 1938.

Einstein, Albert. *Science, Philosophy and Religion: A Symposium*, 1941.

Holy Bible. King James Version.

Qur'án. *The Koran*. Trans. George Sale (1812). Vol. II.

Hubbard, Elbert. 'Little journeys to the homes of great businessmen', www.trussel.com/cooper/pcooper.htm (consulted 10 May 2006).

Marshall, P.J. (ed.). *The Writings and Speeches of Edmund Burke*. Vol. VII: India: The Hastings Trial 1789–1794. Oxford: Clarendon Press, 2000.

Mill, John Stuart. *On Liberty* (1859). London: Penguin Classics, 1975.

Morley, John, Viscount. *On Compromise* (1874). London: Macmillan, 1908.

Mother Earth (1906–17). Ed. Emma Goldman. New York: Greenwood Reprint Corp, 1968.

Mumford, Lewis. *Faith for Living*. New York: Harcourt, Brace, 1940.

The New York Times Magazine, 1902; 9 January 1955; 2 August 1964.

Paine, Thomas. *The Age of Reason: Being an Investigation of True and Fabulous Theology* (Paris: Barrois, 1794). New York: G P. Putnam's Sons, 1896; RP Dover, 2004.

Ruskin, John. *The Crown of Wild Olive*: *Essays on Work, Traffic, War and the Future of England*. London: George Allen & Unwin, 1915.

—. *Time and Tide by Weare and Tyne: Twenty-five Letters to a Working Man of Sunderland on the Laws of Work* (1867). London, George Allen, 1906.

Samuels, Ernest. *Henry Adams: The Middle Years*. Harvard: Belknap, 1958.

Teilhard de Chardin, Pierre. *The Phenomenon of Man* (1955). Trans. Bernard Wall. New York: Harper & Row, rev.ed. 1975.

References

[1] John Ruskin, *The Crown of Wild Olive*, p.185–6.

[2] Dhammapada, v.201; trans. Müller, p. 24 (ch. XV).

[3] 'Abdu'l-Bahá, *Some Answered Questions*, ch. 55: 'Soul, Spirit and Mind'.

[4] Bahá'u'lláh, Súriy-i-Haykal, in *Summons*, p. 82.para. 157.

[5] 'Abdu'l-Bahá, *Some Answered Questions*, ch. 66, pp. 239–40.

[6] ibid. ch. 60, p. 225.

[7] ibid. ch. 63, p. 233.

[8] ibid. ch. 53: 'The Relation between God and the Creature', pp. 202–4. 'Abdu'l-Bahá's explanations clarify this interesting subject.

[9] Bahá'u'lláh, *Gleanings* LXXXII, p. 163, para.11.

[10] 'Abdu'l-Bahá, *Some Answered Questions*, ch. 47, p. 182.

[11] ibid. ch. 59, p. 220.

[12] ibid.

[13] 'Abdu'l-Bahá, *Selections*, no. 201, p. 246.

[14] John 16: 12–13.

[15] Qu'rán 12: 111 (Súrih of Joseph).

[16] Bhagavad Gita, trans. Prabhavananda and Isherwood.

[17] 'Abdu'l-Bahá, *Some Answered Questions*, ch. 41, pp. 161–2.

[18] ibid. ch. 77.

[19] Anguttara Nikaya 1–88.

[20] Bahá'u'lláh, *Gleanings* CXVII, p.250; Hidden Words, Arabic 1.

[21] Teilhard, *The Phenomenon of Man*, Book 4, ch.2, p.265.

[22] ibid. p.264.

[23] Morley, ch.3: 'Intellectual responsibility and the political spirit', para.28.

[24] Mumford, *Faith for Living*, p. 216.

[25] Quoted in Brewster, *Memoirs*, vol. II, ch. 27.

[26] Paine, *Age of Reason*, Part 1, ch.1: 'The author's profession of faith', p.22.

[27] ibid. Part 1, "Recapitulation", pp. 83–4.

[28] Attributed to Renan.

[29] *Time and Tide* (1867), Letter 13.

[30] Attributed to Abd-ar-Rahman III.

[31] Quoted in Samuels, *Henry Adams*.

[32] Comment made by a personal friend as we were discussing these questions.

[33] *L'evolution créative* (Creative Evolution) (1907), ch.1: 'Le présent ne contient rien de plus que le passé, et ce qu'on trouve dans l'effet était déjà dans la cause.'

[34] Address to the Swedish Government Peace Conference, 1909, quoted in *The Saturday Review* (New York), 9 August 1958.

[35] Quoted in *The New York Times Magazine*, 9 January 1955, issue celebrating Schweitzer's 80th birthday.

[36] Quoted in *The Atlantic Monthly*, November 1958. A similar passage is found in Schweitzer's *Aus meinem Leben und Denken* (From my Life and Thought) (1933), ch. 13: ' There flashed upon my mind, unforeseen and unsought, the phrase, "Reverence for Life" (Ehrfurcht vor dem Leben).

[37] Jay Burns Baking Company v. Bryan, quoted in *Opinion*, 1924.

[38] Speech, 28 May 1794, quoted in Bond, vol. 4, p. 377. See also Marshall (ed.), *Writings and Speeches*.

[39] Attributed to Confucius.

[40] Memorial to the Legislature of New York, in Hubbard, 'Little Journeys'.

[41] Einstein, in Lapp, 'The Einstein letter that started it all', in *The New York Times Magazine*, 2 August 1964. 'When he was five years old, Einstein's father gave him a compass. Einstein said that playing with the compass "made a deep and lasting impression on me. Something hidden had to be behind things" '
(www.physicsmatters.org/einstein/compass.htm, consulted 10 May 2006).

[42] Statement to G.S. Viereck, 1921, quoted in Dukas and Hoffmann, p. 38.

[43] Einstein, *Science, Philosophy and Religion*, ch. 13.

[44] From an article contributed by Ferrer to *Mother Earth*. Nov. 1909.

[45] 1902, Quoted in *The New York Times Magazine*.

[46] Mill, *On Liberty*, ch. 1.

[47] Anonymous, often wrongly attributed to Herbert Spencer (1820–1903), English philosopher.

[48] Bahá'u'lláh, Hidden Words, Arabic nos. 3, 4 and 7.